RUGBY
WORLD CUP
2015
THE OFFICIAL
TOURNAMENT GUIDE

First published by Carlton Books Limited in 2015

Copyright © Carlton Books Limited 2015

The words "Rugby World Cup" are protected by Trade Mark and/or Copyright.
TM © Rugby World Cup Limited 1986–2015. All rights reserved.
RWC Font. Copyright © 2008 RWC Ltd. All rights reserved.
Unauthorised use, modification, reproduction and distribution prohibited.
TM © Rugby World Cup Limited 1986–2015. All rights reserved.

Carlton Books Limited
20 Mortimer Street
London W1T 3JW

A CIP catalogue record for this book is available from the British Library.
10 9 8 7 6 5 4 3 2 1

ISBN 978-1-78097-650-1

Project director: Martin Corteel
Project Art Editor: Luke Griffin
Production: Maria Petalidou

Printed in Spain

All statistics correct at January 1, 2015

RUGBY WORLD CUP 2015

THE OFFICIAL TOURNAMENT GUIDE

Foreword by

Bernard Lapasset

World Rugby Chairman

CARLTON
BOOKS

Contents

Foreword

Bernard Lapasset
Chairman, World Rugby

Rugby World Cup 2015 will be a very special and record-breaking celebration of Rugby and its values, furthering the growth of our sport around the globe, and I am delighted that you will be with us on this incredible journey.

In less than three decades, our showcase event has grown from humble beginnings in 1987 to box office hit, reaching out, engaging and inspiring new audiences and participants in record numbers with each edition.

Each has delivered its own unforgettable moments that have gone down in Rugby folklore. Whether it was Nelson Mandela presenting the Webb Ellis Cup to Francois Pienaar in 1995 and, in doing so, uniting a nation, or Jonah Lomu ripping through defences or *that* Jonny Wilkinson drop goal, Rugby World Cups deliver magic in abundance.

England 2015 will be no different. It will be a Tournament that has players and fans at heart and on the field new stars will emerge, showcasing their skills across 13 outstanding packed venues to record television audiences in more countries than ever before.

From the north-east to the south-west and across the Severn Bridge to Cardiff, England 2015 will excite, inspire and touch everyone in the country. Our goal, whether you are a fan at a game, in a fanzone, watching on television or engaging with the Tournament via digital and social media, is to deliver an amazing Rugby World Cup experience.

For World Rugby, England 2015 is more than just a wonderful showcase of Rugby, it is the financial driving force behind the development of the Game and the major source of funding for the 20 competing nations.

Between 2009 and 2016, we are investing more than £330 million in community and high-performance programmes, player welfare and tournaments in order that more teams have the chance to qualify for and win Rugby World Cup.

Rugby is a major growth sport, played by 7.2 million men, women and children worldwide, and we are delighted that we have grown participation by 33 per cent in the last decade. We are committed to accelerating that growth and England 2015 will provide the perfect platform for us to do that.

England 2015 will be good for the sport and good for the Host Nation. It is anticipated that nearly 500,000 travelling fans will visit England and Wales during the Tournament, while the local economy is set to benefit to the tune of £2 billion, making England 2015 the most impactful Rugby World Cup to date.

I know that England will be a wonderful, welcoming host and on behalf of World Rugby, I would like to wish you a memorable Rugby World Cup and thank you for your tremendous support of Rugby around the world.

World Rugby Chairman Bernard Lapasset with the Webb Ellis Cup

Introduction

Rugby World Cup 2015 promises to be a record-breaking celebration of the character-building values that make the game so special – and everyone is invited. The Tournament provides an opportunity to once again demonstrate how the sport has developed since the first Rugby World Cup was held in New Zealand and Australia in 1987.

In less than three decades, the event has become one of the biggest and best-loved sporting occasions on the planet and England – the birthplace of Rugby – will be a fitting stage.

The 2012 Olympic Games in London highlighted the passion the English public has for sport, whether cheering on their own team, witnessing superstars on home soil, or getting behind the underdogs.

That will once again be the case at Rugby World Cup 2015 and the unprecedented level of demand for tickets ever since they went on sale highlighted the enthusiasm for the eighth staging of the event. Fans from the UK and around the planet scrambled to get their hands on a prized ticket to ensure entry at one of the 48 matches, proving that Rugby World Cup 2015 is too big to miss. More than five million ticket applications were received during the 17-day application window and record sales through official travel and hospitality programmes and packages illustrate the interest the Tournament has generated not just in the UK but around the world too.

On the pitch, the battle to be crowned world champions once again promises to be intriguing right through until the full-time whistle is blown at Twickenham on October 31. Having waited so long to regain the trophy after a 24-year drought, New Zealand will be desperate to keep the Webb Ellis Cup and prove they are undoubtedly the best team in world Rugby. Success at this level does not come easy though and they will face fierce competition.

England are hoping to repeat their Jonny Wilkinson-inspired heroics of 2003 and France are desperate to finally get their hands on the silverware after finishing runners-up three times. New Zealand's southern hemisphere rivals, South Africa and Australia, should again be in contention and Wales and Ireland cannot be written off. For other teams, just being part of the event is success in itself and they will enjoy the chance to test themselves on Rugby's biggest stage.

Rugby World Cup 2015: The Official Guide has all the information a Rugby fan could need ahead of the Tournament. It features a profile of the teams and potential stars, a guide to the venues, a review of how the countries qualified, a look back at the seven previous Tournaments and a summary of some of the records which are waiting to be broken as the next chapter in Rugby World Cup history is written.

All Blacks prop Tony Woodcock dives over for the only try of the Rugby World Cup 2011 Final as New Zealand beat France in Auckland. Now they are out to retain their title and win the Webb Ellis Cup on foreign soil for the first time

Above: England number 8 Ben Morgan is congratulated after scoring a try against Australia at Twickenham, where the two sides will do battle again in Pool A on October 3

Left: The statue of William Webb Ellis in the grounds of Rugby School

Top right: The fans' experience has been at the heart of planning for Rugby World Cup 2015 in England

Right: The Webb Ellis Cup on show at Rugby School, the Warwickshire public school to which the Game traces its history

WELCOME
TO ENGLAND

England is widely acknowledged as Rugby's birthplace. Legend has it that William Webb Ellis picked up the ball and ran with it at Rugby School in 1823, with the Game's most prestigious Trophy named after him. Venue for many celebrated post-war sporting occasions, such as the 1948 and 2012 Olympics and football's World Cup in 1966, visitors to England are assured of a brilliant, breathtaking Rugby World Cup 2015 spectacle across the length and breadth of its famous landscape.

About Rugby World Cup 2015

The eighth edition of Rugby World Cup promises to be bigger and better than ever before and it seems everyone wants a piece of the action. Unprecedented demand for tickets and interest in being a volunteer have highlighted the excitement around the sporting climax of the year.

Mayor of London Boris Johnson and England 2015 Ambassador Lawrence Dallaglio

It is gearing up to be the biggest global sporting spectacle of the year, a feast of Rugby to inspire the world. The organisers of Rugby World Cup 2015 in England and Wales have set themselves ambitious targets, not least for this Tournament to go down as the greatest in its history.

The signs have been overwhelmingly positive – the demand for tickets exceeded even the most optimistic predictions, thousands of people put their names forward to become volunteers, while on the field of play itself the excitement has been building with several sides viewed as being in with a chance of being crowned world champions at Twickenham on Saturday, October 31.

The vision of the organisers has been to deliver a Tournament that celebrates Rugby and its values, and to inspire the nation and the world. The aim has been to "welcome the world", and that is certainly set to be the case. Research figures show 400,000 to 500,000 people will come in to the country for the Tournament and the detailed plans in place should ensure that fans, media, sponsors, officials and, of course, the players all have a fantastic experience at Rugby World Cup 2015.

Over 1.9 million tickets have been sold for the Tournament with prices starting from as little as £7 for a child and £15 for an adult, putting it well within the price range for a family

Madagascar – which has adopted Rugby as its national sport – displayed the Webb Ellis Cup to excited children at the Father Pedro Foundation

day out. The initial ticket sales launch astounded the organisers as close to a million tickets were snapped up and every single match saw at least one ticket category over-subscribed. England's match against Australia at Twickenham, on October 3, attracted more than 650,000 applications.

There was never any doubt that there would be huge demand for England matches at Twickenham but less predictable was the worldwide response when the tickets went on general sale. Regardless of the venue, whether it was Leeds, Newcastle, Cardiff, Gloucester or Exeter, fans were

keen to get a close-up view of the action. Historically, matches between outsiders for the knock-out stages are often very exciting and evoke the whole spirit of the Tournament and clearly the spectators have bought into that.

The first steps towards the competition began back in May 2014, when the famous Webb Ellis Cup – Rugby's most coveted prize – set off on an International Trophy Tour covering tens of thousands of miles, from the heartlands of Rugby-mad nations to countries it has never been before. From Madagascar, the island country off the continent of Africa

which has just adopted Rugby as its national sport, to the United Arab Emirates, Romania and China, the Webb Ellis Cup has been finding new friends and fans of Rugby ahead of the Tournament itself. After visiting 15 countries, the trophy will come to England, Scotland, Wales, Northern Ireland and the Republic of Ireland en route to the opening match on September 18.

Any major sporting event relies on volunteers and Rugby World Cup 2015 will be no exception. There will be some 6,000 volunteers and to recognise those who support the

game week-in week-out, England Rugby 2015 has been working with clubs across the country to ensure that those involved in delivering the game at grassroots level are rewarded with the chance to be part of Rugby's biggest event.

The foundations are all in place for a wonderful Rugby World Cup 2015, but organisers will focus until the very end on all the nuts and bolts that will raise it from a good Tournament to a great one, including the long-term legacy. This includes putting the players at the heart of the planning – the training camps, the travel times to matches, commercial opportunities, provisions for supporters

in terms of big screens, eating and drinking, fan zones and security.

The organisers have been able to take plenty of lessons from the London Olympics, knowing that there can never be too much planning and too much testing when staging an event of this size. The spectator experience is central to much of the planning, ensuring the unforgettable moments are fully enjoyed and appreciated whether it is a fan in the stadium or watching on television.

Another key aspect of the planning for the Tournament is what it leaves behind for the sport. The legacy issue was highlighted time and again in the

build-up to London 2012 and it will be no different – but perhaps easier – for Rugby World Cup 2015, given there is one sport to focus on rather than the 26 involved at the London 2012 Olympics. The Rugby Football Union has a seven-point legacy programme and Rugby World Cup 2015 organisers will be helping to deliver that, whether it is across participation or encouraging more girls to play or improving facilities. The aim is to have more people engaged in the Game, whether it is playing or coaching or volunteering or simply just watching.

For World Rugby, the global governing body of the sport, Rugby World Cup

The Webb Ellis Cup reaches the most southerly point of Africa, Cape Agulhas, during the International Trophy Tour, accompanied by Rugby World Cup 1995 winner Chester Williams (right) and Rugby World Cup 2007 winning captain John Smit

will be the engine that drives the sport and provides the income to be injected back into the game.

World Rugby chairman Bernard Lapasset states: "Rugby World Cup is all about the fans and the players, and it is our belief that Rugby World Cup 2015 will be a very special record-breaking celebration of Rugby and the host nation." It really is going to be too big to miss.

KNOW THE GAME

POOL PHASE

The Tournament's 20 nations have been drawn into four pools of five teams. Each team will play the other teams in its pool on a round-robin basis. The following number of points will be awarded for each match:
• Win: 4 points
• Draw: 2 points
• Loss: 0 points
• 4 or more tries: 1 point
• Loss by 7 points or less: 1 point

At the completion of the pool phase, the teams in a pool are ranked one to five based on their cumulative match points, and identified respectively as winner, runner-up, third, fourth and fifth. The winner and runner-up in each pool qualify for the quarter-finals. If at the completion of the pool phase two or more teams are level on match points, then the following criteria shall be used in the following order until one of the teams can be determined as the higher ranked:
• The winner of the match in which the two tied teams have played each other shall be the higher ranked;
• The team which has the best difference between points scored for and points scored against in all its pool matches shall be the higher ranked;
• The team which has the best difference between tries scored for and tries scored against in all its pool matches shall be the higher ranked;
• The team which has scored most points in all its pool matches shall be the higher ranked;
• The team which has scored most tries in all its pool matches shall be the higher ranked;
• Should the tie be unresolved at the conclusion of steps one to five, the rankings as per the updated official World Rugby Rankings on October 12, 2015, will determine the higher ranked team.

KNOCKOUT MATCHES

If teams are tied at full-time, the winner shall be determined through the following sequential criteria;
• **Extra time:** Following an interval of five minutes, extra time of 10 minutes each way (with an interval of five minutes) shall be played in full.
• **Sudden death:** If the scores are tied at the conclusion of extra time, and following an interval of five minutes, then a further extra time of 10 minutes maximum shall be played. During this period the first team to score any points shall be declared the winner.
• **Kicking competition:** If after the sudden death period no winner can be declared, a kicking competition will be organised between the two teams. The winner of that competition shall be declared the winner of the match.

QUARTER-FINALS

The top two teams from each pool will progress to the last eight and the quarter-final line-ups will be determined in the following way:
• **QF1:** Winner Pool B v Runner-up Pool A
• **QF2:** Winner Pool C v Runner-up Pool D
• **QF3:** Winner Pool D v Runner-up Pool C
• **QF4:** Winner Pool A v Runner-up Pool B

SEMI-FINALS

The semi-final line-ups will be decided in the following manner:
• **SF1:** Winner QF1 v Winner QF2
• **SF2:** Winner QF3 v Winner QF4

BRONZE FINAL

This match will be contested between the two losing semi-finalists.

THE FINAL

This match will be contested between the two winning semi-finalists.

England: The Birthplace of Rugby

Nobody could have predicted the consequences when schoolboy William Webb Ellis is said to have picked up the ball and set off running at Rugby School almost two centuries ago, but now the sport of Rugby is returning to its birthplace as England stages Rugby World Cup 2015.

A sense of Rugby Union coming home will resound around Twickenham when England host Fiji in the opening match of Rugby World Cup 2015. While different forms of football in which the ball was handled existed across the globe for centuries before William Webb Ellis is said to have intervened in 1823, it was the spread of the new code across the English public school system in the 19th century that gave birth to the Game as it is now known.

Early versions of the sport were viewed with suspicion by authorities during the Middle Ages to the extent that they were often banned, but by the 1800s they were accepted as a useful outlet for the exuberance of public school students. There was no overall cohesion, though, as rules varied from school to school and were made up by the pupils themselves.

Rugby had its true genesis in the midlands of England at the synonymous Rugby School and was born out of a version recorded in 1817 that allowed boys to catch the ball but prohibited running forwards with it. That changed in 1823 with the story of the 16-year-old Webb Ellis gathering the ball into his arms and charging upfield. Whether accurate or embellished, he has a place in Rugby folklore and the Rugby World Cup Trophy bears his name.

The name Webb Ellis remains inextricably linked to the founding of the Game, but the authenticity of his tale has never been verified. The story's origins were letters sent to the Rugby

England against Scotland is the oldest fixture in international rugby, dating back to the first meeting in March 1871

School paper by Matthew Bloxham that outlined Webb Ellis' involvement, though through nothing more than the eye-witness account of an unnamed source. Casting further doubt on the story was confusion over the year when Bloxham said Webb Ellis first picked up the ball. Whatever the truth, Webb Ellis has been immortalised and to this day a plaque in honour of the famed former student is in place at Rugby School. It reads: "This stone commemorates the exploit of William Webb Ellis who with a fine disregard for the rules of football as played in his time first took the ball in his arms and ran with it thus originating the distinctive feature of the Rugby game AD 1823".

Running with the ball caught on and soon became a feature of the Game, which was graced with its first set of rules – 37 in total – by Rugby School in 1845. As pupils graduated, Rugby spread with some establishing clubs in England and others taking it overseas.

The team formed by Guy's Hospital in London is recognised by the Rugby Football Union and *Guinness Book of Records* as the oldest Rugby club in the world. The expansion of the Game was affected by the disparity over rules, with different schools and clubs having their own variations. This issue was rectified in January 1871 with the formation of the Rugby Football Union in London. Five months later, a trio of former Rugby School pupils drew up the rules after being tasked by committee to give the Game the structure it

The statue of William Webb Ellis in the grounds of Rugby School in Warwickshire

needed. The first international match was played in March of that year when the Scottish and English members of the RFU organised a fixture that was played in Edinburgh in front of a 4,000 crowd. Scotland won the game by one goal at a time when matches could only be decided by kicking. The objective of scoring a try was in order to set up the conversion and it was points secured from these that settled the outcome in a system that was to remain in place until the late 1880s.

Mondays were the day used to stage games in the infancy of international Rugby and each side contained 20 players, including a forward pack of 13. By 1875, forward-thinking advocates of the Game experimented with a reduction in numbers that quickly caught on, partly because teams of 15 were easier to assemble than teams of 20.

The remaining home unions were set up soon after the first international game – Scotland in 1873, Ireland in 1879 and Wales in 1880. The 1882-83

season produced a first Triple Crown, with England claiming that honour after toppling their Celtic rivals. The creation of the International Rugby Board swiftly followed, formed by Scotland, Ireland and Wales in 1886. Having initially rejected the opportunity to join the new body – and missing out on international fixtures against their home union rivals as a result – England relented four years later. All members agreed in 1930 that the IRB would retain sole jurisdiction over the rules.

By 1893 a division had appeared in the Game. A proposal for players to be paid to compensate for time lost at work began to gather support, but this contravened the Game's strict amateur code. The motion was outvoted at an RFU annual general meeting, resulting in the creation of the Northern Union – later to become Rugby League – by clubs from Cheshire, Yorkshire and Lancashire in 1895. A century later, the Game followed in league's footsteps by becoming professional after the IRB

made its famous declaration in 1995 that it was now 'open'.

The first international staged at Twickenham was in January 1910 when Wales were defeated 11-6, ending a nomadic spell for the RFU during which English Rugby suffered from the split that had torn the Game asunder. England's pack had suffered in particular, losing the hard men supplied from the strongholds of Yorkshire and Lancashire after those counties had chosen to navigate their own course through the sporting landscape. Adding to the importance of 1910 was that it was the first time France competed against each of the home unions, giving birth to the first Five Nations Championship, a tournament that endures to this day with the addition of Italy in 2000 increasing the number of competing teams to six.

Although still in its infancy, Rugby was expanding at an impressive rate and some names now synonymous with the sport began to appear. The British and Irish Lions would not be formalised for some time, but the famed tourists set out on their maiden voyage in 1888 as a private-enterprise trip to Australia and New Zealand. Led by Alfred Shaw and Arthur Shrewsbury, famous England cricketers, there was also an Ashes tour to Australia, the rugby team contained mainly England players, but there was also a Scottish and Welsh presence. No (Rugby) Tests were played on the daunting 35-match tour, and 19 of the matches involved a form of Australian Rules football. The 1891 South Africa tour was the first officially-sanctioned Lions trip. South Africa played a key role during the Lions' development years, welcoming them again in 1896, and by the time Australia was revisited in 1899 the tourists were a genuine mix of representatives from all four home unions. It was on the 1950 tour to New Zealand and Australia that the elite of British and Irish rugby became officially known as the Lions.

The Barbarians, another name inextricably linked to Rugby, were conceived by WP Carpmael in April 1890

England coach Stuart Lancaster is a keen student of the history of the Game

A plaque at Rugby School commemorates England's Rugby World Cup win in 2003

philosophy, Lancaster has researched the connection New Zealand's players have with their jerseys. It was noted by the former schoolteacher that England's rivals – nations such as Wales, South Africa and Scotland – are able to draw on history and past deeds to drive performance. Perceiving this to be missing with England, he has recognised the need to embrace the past to help his current squad appreciate the depth and significance of their modern-day roles.

"We've been going through the process of recapturing our own sense of heritage – of discovering what the England shirt means," Lancaster said. "When the All Blacks were in transition in the middle years of the last decade, they really understood how powerful a source of motivation the history of the shirt could be. Identity is a complex subject for us. We're an island nation, made up of different Rugby nations. But we've been talking about what links the shirt to the history of the England team and the next step is to make a full connection with the country at large."

Several innovations have been introduced, among them the Arthur Harrison Award where England coaches select a winner after every match for the player producing the best defensive performance. Harrison is England's only Rugby international to have been awarded the Victoria Cross, bestowed posthumously after he lost his life in the Zeebrugge raid of April 1918 in the First World War. Every player is made aware of the history of their jersey. Above each peg in the home dressing room at Twickenham is a list of those who have filled the position before.

Lancaster has also addressed his squad on the story of England's first black player, James Peters. He was a dockyard worker who won the first of his five caps in 1907 and his story was deemed pertinent by Lancaster because of his squad's multi-cultural make-up.

There is much for English Rugby to be proud of and the latest chapter in its long, colourful history will be written when Rugby World Cup 2015 highlights how much the Game has developed since the days of Webb Ellis.

at a hotel in Bradford. Membership was by invitation only with the philosophy behind the team being to spread camaraderie among all Rugby players. Their first fixture was a 9-4 victory over Hartlepool Rovers in December that year and they became known for their swashbuckling style, which holds true to this day. The relevance of the Barbarians in the professional era may be uncertain, but their games continue to throw up some thrilling encounters.

Rugby spread across the globe rapidly with eager early adopters taking it to parts of the British Empire and British colonies, while those visitors to the United Kingdom and Ireland who had enjoyed their first experience of the Game spread the word on their return home. Unions were quickly set up with New Zealand and South Africa establishing theirs at the end of the 19th century and Australia following

suit, although with a precursor to what is now known as the Australian Rugby Union. Argentina was added to the list and in the early decades of the following century Fiji, Tonga, Samoa and Japan created their own unions.

The first tour to England unfolded in 1888-89 when what is now known as the Maori All Blacks travelled the country playing a large number of games. Their visit was not without mishap though after the international against England became mired in an unseemly refereeing controversy.

The heritage of English Rugby has become an important feature of the current national set-up overseen by head coach Stuart Lancaster. He has repeatedly invoked England's rich Rugby history since replacing Martin Johnson in 2011, using it to inject a sense of national pride in his players. A keen student of the All Blacks and their

Match Venues

Thirteen venues across 10 English cities plus the Welsh capital of Cardiff have been chosen to host the 48 matches at Rugby World Cup 2015. Dedicated Rugby stadia will stage 25 games while multi-event stadia and football venues will also help to provide more than two million opportunities for fans to watch the action.

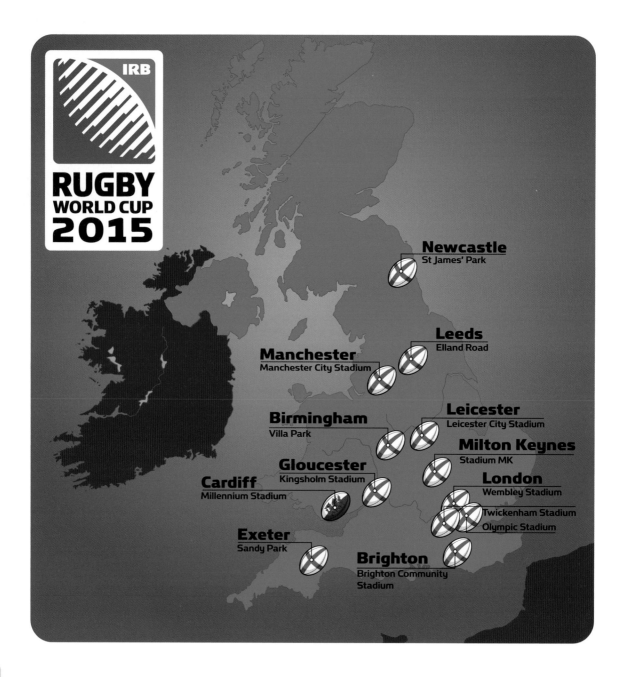

TWICKENHAM STADIUM, LONDON

Capacity: 81,605

Matches hosted:

England v Fiji	(A, Sept 18)
France v Italy	(D, Sept 19)
England v Wales	(A, Sept 26)
England v Australia	(A, Oct 3)
Australia v Wales	(A, Oct 10)
Quarter-final 2	(Oct 17)
Quarter-final 4	(Oct 18)
Semi-final 1	(Oct 24)
Semi-final 2	(Oct 25)
Rugby World Cup Final	(Oct 31)

The home of English Rugby is the largest dedicated Rugby venue in the world and the perfect stage for 10 matches, including both semi-finals and the October 31 climax. A former cabbage patch, Rugby has been played here since 1909 when local teams Harlequins and Richmond did battle. The iconic venue has hosted numerous memorable matches since, including the Rugby World Cup 1991 Final in which Australia beat England 12-6.

Twickenham Stadium will host 10 matches, including the Rugby World Cup 2015 Final

MILLENNIUM STADIUM, CARDIFF

Capacity: 74,154

Matches hosted:

Ireland v Canada	(D, Sept 19)
Wales v Uruguay	(A, Sept 20)
Australia v Fiji	(A, Sept 23)
Wales v Fiji	(A, Oct 1)
New Zealand v Georgia	(C, Oct 2)
France v Ireland	(D, Oct 11)
Quarter-final 1	(Oct 17)
Quarter-final 3	(Oct 18)

The Millennium Stadium is one of two venues being used in 2015 which has previously hosted a Rugby World Cup Final, having been the setting for Australia's 1999 success against France. Situated on the banks of the River Taff in the Welsh capital, the stadium was the first in the UK to be built with a fully-retractable roof, ensuring no occasion is ruined by the weather and allowing a wide variety of events to be staged.

WEMBLEY STADIUM, LONDON

Capacity: 90,000

Matches hosted:

New Zealand v Argentina	(C, Sept 20)
Ireland v Romania	(D, Sept 27)

Wembley is the largest venue being used for Rugby World Cup 2015, with 90,000 seats spread over three tiers. The stadium reopened in 2007 after being completely rebuilt, with the famous twin towers being replaced by a 133-metre tall arch which is visible across London. Wembley – named after the north London suburb in which it is located – is home to England's national football team but hosts many other major sporting events.

An aerial view of Wembley Stadium in London

OLYMPIC STADIUM, LONDON

Capacity: 54,000

Matches hosted:

France v Romania	(D, Sept 23)
New Zealand v Namibia	(C, Sept 24)
Ireland v Italy	(D, Oct 4)
South Africa v USA	(B, Oct 7)
Bronze Final	(Oct 30)

This venue has already witnessed some iconic sporting moments after being used as the centrepiece for the London 2012 Olympic Games, when the likes of Usain Bolt, Mo Farah and Jessica Ennis shone on the track. It is the third largest stadium in England to be used for Rugby World Cup 2015 and will host four pool matches, as well as the Bronze Final, before becoming home to West Ham United and UK Athletics at a later date.

MANCHESTER CITY STADIUM, MANCHESTER

Capacity: 47,800

Matches hosted:

England v Uruguay	(A, Oct 10)

Built for the 2002 Commonwealth Games, this was the venue for the Rugby Sevens final as New Zealand beat Fiji to claim gold. The stadium is no stranger to sporting drama, having seen Manchester City clinch the Premier League title in the dying minutes of the final match of the season in 2012, and it regularly plays host to Rugby League's Magic Weekend as well as music concerts.

St James' Park, Newcastle

The Olympic Stadium in Stratford, east London, will stage the Bronze Final on October 30

ST JAMES' PARK, NEWCASTLE

Capacity: 52,409

Matches hosted:

South Africa v Scotland	(B, Oct 3)
New Zealand v Tonga	(C, Oct 9)
Samoa v Scotland	(B, Oct 10)

Home to Newcastle United and the club's passionate fans, St James' Park has hosted international competition before as a football venue for the 2012 Olympic Games and at Euro 96. It is the second biggest sports ground in England outside of London and the oldest football stadium in the north-east of England. It was built on the site of an execution gallows, hence the name of the famous Gallowgate End.

ELLAND ROAD, LEEDS

Capacity: 37,914

Matches hosted:

Italy v Canada	(D, Sept 26)
Scotland v USA	(B, Sept 27)

The city of Leeds is better known for its football team, while rugby league giants Leeds Rhinos are based down the road at Headingley, but Elland Road will be a fitting stage for two pool matches. Only one Rugby Union match has previously been played here, with more than 14,000 spectators turning up to see South Africa beat a North of England XV in 1992 shortly after the Springboks were readmitted to the international game.

LEICESTER CITY STADIUM, LEICESTER

Capacity: 32,312

Matches hosted:

Argentina v Tonga	(C, Oct 4)
Canada v Romania	(D, Oct 6)
Argentina v Namibia	(C, Oct 11)

The stadium was opened in the summer of 2002 and is an impressive, state-of-the-art facility which was built to replace Leicester City's former home at Filbert Street. Leicester Tigers have played several Rugby fixtures at the venue, including a Heineken Cup semi-final victory over Llanelli in 2007. In 2006, to celebrate the centenary of Springbok overseas tours, the stadium hosted a World XV v South Africa game, which the Springboks won 32-7.

VILLA PARK, BIRMINGHAM

Capacity: 42,785

Matches hosted:

South Africa v Samoa	(B, Sept 26)
Australia v Uruguay	(A, Sept 27)

Opened in 1897, the home of Aston Villa has held international football matches across three different centuries as well as cycling, boxing, athletics and a number of music concerts, while two Rugby touring sides have played here. A North Midlands select side lost 40-3 against New Zealand in 1924, and in 1953 a Midlands County XV were beaten 18-3 by a Kiwi outfit which included legendary All Blacks Bob Stuart, Richard White and Peter Jones.

KINGSHOLM STADIUM, GLOUCESTER

Capacity: 16,500

Matches hosted:

Tonga v Georgia	(C, Sept 19)
Scotland v Japan	(B, Sept 23)
Argentina v Georgia	(C, Sept 25)
USA v Japan	(B, Oct 11)

Renowned for its vibrant atmosphere, which six different teams will sample during Rugby World Cup 2015, Gloucester's home ground hosted its first Test in 1900 when Wales beat England 13-3. It was 91 years before international Rugby returned during Rugby World Cup 1991 as 12,000 fans saw world champions New Zealand score eight tries as they cruised past the USA 46-6.

STADIUM MK, MILTON KEYNES

Capacity: 30,717

Matches hosted:

France v Canada	(D, Oct 1)
Samoa v Japan	(B, Oct 3)
Fiji v Uruguay	(A, Oct 6)

Northampton and Saracens have hosted fixtures at the football venue, which became home to MK Dons in 2007 when they relocated and changed their name from Wimbledon. Northampton used the stadium for the knockout stages of their Heineken Cup campaign in 2010/11 and rewarded big crowds by beating Ulster and Perpignan in the quarter-finals and semi-finals before losing to Leinster in the Final at the Millennium Stadium.

BRIGHTON COMMUNITY STADIUM, BRIGHTON

Capacity: 30,750

Matches hosted:

South Africa v Japan	(B, Sept 19)
Samoa v USA	(B, Sept 20)

Brighton and Hove Albion's football ground finally opened in 2011 at a cost of £93 million after a lengthy and controversial planning process. Capacity has been gradually increased since then and it is a fitting new home for the club, who had been playing temporarily at the Withdean Stadium after leaving their historic home at the Goldstone Ground. It is situated near the village of Falmer and boasts an eye-catching design with semi-circular stand roofs and tubular supporting steelwork.

SANDY PARK, EXETER

Capacity: 12,300

Matches hosted:

Tonga v Namibia	(C, Sept 29)
Namibia v Georgia	(C, Oct 7)
Italy v Romania	(D, Oct 11)

The home of Exeter Chiefs and the club's vociferous support was built to replace the County Ground in 2006 and has recently undergone multi-million pound redevelopments. It is due to expand further to 20,600 after Rugby World Cup 2015 which will see it become one of the biggest club grounds in England. It is located just off the M5 motorway, has good rail links and is only 10 minutes away from Exeter Airport.

Gloucester's Kingsholm Stadium is famed for its atmosphere and will host four games at Rugby World Cup 2015

CAPTAIN KIRK'S ENTERPRISE
JUNE 20, 1987, EDEN PARK, AUCKLAND

David Kirk became the first captain to hold the Webb Ellis Cup aloft when co-hosts New Zealand won the inaugural Rugby World Cup in 1987. The whole country was at fever pitch after the All Blacks had made it through to the Final at Auckland's Eden Park to meet a France side who were full of confidence after winning an epic semi-final against Australia. The tension of the occasion before a sell-out crowd of 48,000 was reflected by a tight first half in which New Zealand led 9-0 and France could not get their free-flowing running game going. Scrum-half Kirk then settled home nerves when he broke off the back of a ruck and took a pass from Michael Jones to dive over in the corner, New Zealand eventually running out clear 29-9 winners.

All Blacks captain David Kirk lifts the Webb Ellis Cup after victory over France

Above: The United States qualified for Rugby World Cup 2015 with a play-off win over Uruguay, who ultimately joined them via the Repechage

Left: England's bid team, including Rugby World Cup 2003 winners Lawrence Dallaglio (left) and Will Greenwood (centre), arrive for the bid presentation in Dublin

Right: New Zealand's mighty All Blacks will arrive at Rugby World Cup 2015 as the world's number one ranked team

THE ROAD TO ENGLAND

The long and winding road to Rugby World Cup 2015 reached journey's end one year before the Tournament when its 20th and final place was filled. Uruguay were the last of eight teams to successfully come through the qualifying process and secure their trip to England, who were announced as the host nation in Dublin back in 2009. This section also looks at the World Rugby Rankings heading into a crucial year of Rugby.

How England's bid was won

The right to stage Rugby World Cup 2015 was understandably fiercely contested and South Africa and Italy both made impressive bids but, at a World Rugby meeting in Dublin in 2009, it was announced that England would become the outright hosts of the Tournament for the first time.

Each bidding country developed a comprehensive programme outlining exactly how they would stage the Tournament. This included details of where the matches would be held, the facilities available to provide training bases for the competing teams, commercial opportunities, provisions for supporters in terms of big screens and fan zones, ticket plans and, perhaps most importantly of all, their plans for the legacy impact of staging Rugby World Cup 2015 in terms of the

development of the sport beyond the staging of the Tournament itself.

South Africa were hoping to build on the wonderful memories of their hosting of Rugby World Cup 1995, which had delivered not just an unforgettable Tournament but one of the most momentous occasions in that country's sporting history when Nelson Mandela, the first black President of South Africa, donned a Springboks shirt before the Final to help bury the divisions of apartheid and inspire the

team of the new Rainbow Nation to victory over New Zealand.

For Italy, the country was hoping to stage Rugby World Cup for the first time, a powerful argument for World Rugby to consider, given its commitment to spreading the sport further across the globe. England had been co-hosts in 1991, which was only the second Rugby World Cup following its launch four years before. Since then the status of the Tournament had grown enormously to become one of

Rugby World Cup 2003 winner Jonny Wilkinson teams up with Prince Harry at Rugby School to mark one year to go to England 2015

THE RFU LEGACY PLAN

FACILITIES
The RFU has committed an investment of £10m to create £25m worth of improvements in club equipment and facilities benefiting more than 500 clubs nationwide – from kit and equipment to clubhouses, changing rooms and floodlights to all-weather pitches.

PEOPLE
New investment of more than £1m to deliver more than 6,500 newly-qualified referees and coaches. Staging masterclasses for more than 5,000 existing coaches and referees along with a focus on young people, bringing in 5,000 additional club volunteers.

SCHOOLS
The RFU's All Schools programme will ensure more schools are offering Rugby and will give more than one million young people opportunities to play. The initiative aims to introduce the game into 400 non-Rugby playing secondary schools by 2015 and up to 750 by 2019, by delivering a package of resources within the school.

RETURNING PLAYERS
Working with colleges, universities and employers to inspire thousands of 16-24-year-old players back into clubs across England.

TOUCH RUGBY
Ambition to encourage 15,000 new players to take up Rugby by broadening the reach and appeal of the game through more access to Touch Rugby. more than 200 club-based and 100 university-based centres will be set up by 2015, offering a range of pitch up and play activity, organised leagues and events.

OTHER NATIONS
Building links between the RFU's Constituent Bodies and more than 15 of Europe's key developing Rugby nations to share knowledge on how best to grow and develop the Game throughout the continent.

CULTURAL ENGAGEMENT
Developing a series of cultural programmes using art and photography to bring alive what Rugby means to local communities, encouraging people across the country to talk about the Game.

the top three biggest sports events alongside the Olympic Games and soccer's World Cup.

England outlined a desire to stage the "biggest and best Rugby World Cup ever", and one that would not just benefit the sport across Britain, but would spread Rugby's message across the world. The commercial possibilities would also allow World Rugby to grow the Game globally in an unprecedented fashion, said England's bid team.

The tension was palpable as the bidding countries gathered in Dublin on July 28, 2009 for a meeting at the Royal College of Physicians that would determine the outcome of the contest.

South Africa's bid leader Mark Alexander was in buoyant mood ahead of the vote, saying: "The requirements are shaped to the commercial and developmental needs of the Game and we believe that South Africa offers not only a guaranteed financial success but also a significant dividend in terms of Rugby development that cannot be easily overlooked."

Rugby World Cup Limited had commissioned analysis of all bids by sports business experts Deloittes, marketing and broadcasting giants IMG and legal firm Clifford Chance. Their recommendations were made to the World Rugby Council ahead of the vote. England's bid had the strongest financial cases and was projected to generate some £300 million for World Rugby, who would be able to use much of that for development of the Game.

After presentations from all the bidding countries, World Rugby's 26-man council voted 16-10 in favour of accepting the recommended package of England as hosts for Rugby World Cup 2015, with Japan staging the Tournament in 2019. If there was disappointment in South Africa and Italy, the announcement was greeted with joy in England. The then Prime Minister Gordon Brown stated: "Rugby World Cup 2015 is yet another tremendous event to add to the country's decade of sport and another chance to show our nation's passion for sport and what world-class facilities we have to offer. I'm sure the whole country will want to play their part in making this the most memorable of Rugby World Cups."

World Rugby's vice-chairman Bill Beaumont, the former England captain, also welcomed the news from a global perspective, saying: "It will do a huge amount for the global game. The finances by hosting the competition in England are significant. That will then enable World Rugby to grow the game because 95 per cent of all World Rugby's income comes from Rugby World Cup. It is important we have a successful financial Tournament. It will be a great showcase for the Game because there are some iconic stadia being used and I think you will get a real buy-in from everyone in the UK."

For the winning bid, though, there was little time to celebrate: the planning for the biggest Rugby World Cup ever started immediately and it is all now about to come to fruition.

How they qualified

Mexico City and Montevideo may be cities more renowned for their footballing heritage but the capitals of Mexico and Uruguay provided the book-ends for a Rugby World Cup 2015 qualification process which featured 83 nations across six continents, competing in no fewer than 203 matches.

Namibia advanced from the African qualifying competition with victory over Madagascar

The long road to England began with the first Rugby World Cup 2015 qualifying match between Mexico and Jamaica in March 2012, only five months and one day after the Webb Ellis Cup had been hoisted aloft by New Zealand captain Richie McCaw after the 2011 Final.

Two years, six months and 17 days later, at the end of the qualifying process, Uruguay became the 20th and final team to seal their place at the eighth edition of the Tournament.

The first Test of the global qualifying process, which was won 68-14 by Mexico, was officiated by Craig Joubert, the South African referee who had overseen the All Blacks' victory in the 2011 Final in Auckland only five months previously.

The top three teams in each pool at Rugby World Cup 2011 secured automatic qualification for England 2015 as a result of their efforts in New Zealand, meaning Scotland could at least take some solace from being eliminated at the pool stages for the first time. Tonga, Italy and Samoa were the other teams who missed out on a quarter-final place but who could already begin planning their next Rugby World Cup mission.

Mexico and Jamaica started the race for the remaining eight qualification spots, 153 days after the All Blacks had sealed their 2011 triumph on home soil. The teams who met in Mexico City did not do enough to advance, but Uruguay did. Los Teros had been beaten by a point by Russia in Krasnoyarsk, but responded with a 36-27 victory at the Estadio Charrúa to seal a 57-49 aggregate success in front of 14,000 spectators, with Uruguay President Jose Mujica among them. The Repechage Final victory saw Uruguay advance to a first Rugby World Cup in 12 years and a third in all, following their appearances at the 1999 and 2003 editions.

Uruguay had an earlier opportunity to reach England 2015, but fell to the United States in a closely-fought two-legged play-off. The South Americans had beaten Brazil and Chile to earn the right to challenge the USA, beaten by Canada, for a place at Rugby World Cup 2015. The United States' victory saw them take their place in Pool B and Uruguay fell into the Repechage.

Hong Kong were dispatched in the semi-final before the two-legged contest with Russia decided the final team to play at the Tournament. Russia had put in some spirited performances at the 2011 event but will be absent this time as Uruguay overcame a one-point deficit from the away leg to take up a place in Pool A, with fly-half Felipe Berchesi kicking 21 points for the hosts in the second leg.

Fiji's place was secured with a 17-try defeat of the Cook Islands, who had prevailed from a tournament involving Papua New Guinea, Solomon Islands and Tahiti to reach the Oceania play-off. The Cook Islands were no match for Fiji, who won 108-6 to ensure their proud record of appearing at every Rugby World Cup remained intact. The victory also earned Fiji the honour of playing England in the opening match of Rugby World Cup 2015 at Twickenham on September 18.

Japan, like Fiji, advanced to an eighth Rugby World Cup, qualifying as Asia's representatives to join the United States in Pool B. The Brave Blossoms won the Asian Five Nations, sealing their place at England 2015 with a 49-8 defeat of Hong Kong in Tokyo.

Africa will be represented by South Africa and Namibia, who missed the

QUALIFYING PROGRAMME

REGIONAL QUALIFICATION

Region	Number of teams
AFRICA	12
Qualifiers: Namibia	
Repechage: Zimbabwe	
AMERICAS	18
Qualifiers: Canada	
United States	
Repechage: Uruguay	
ASIA	17
Qualifiers: Japan	
Repechage: Hong Kong	
EUROPE	31
Qualifiers: Georgia	
Romania	
Repechage: Russia	
OCEANIA	5
Qualifiers: Fiji	
Repechage: None	

REPECHAGE RESULTS
Semi-finals

Russia	23-15	Zimbabwe
Uruguay	28-3	Hong Kong

Final

Russia	22-21	Uruguay
Uruguay	36-27	Russia

Uruguay won 57-49 on aggregate

first three editions of Rugby World Cup, but have been ever-present since, although they secured a fifth successive place at the Tournament in dramatic fashion.

Zimbabwe and Kenya, who had narrowly beaten Namibia, were in pole position on the final day of the Africa Cup but neither side could claim a bonus point in Zimbabwe's defeat of Kenya.

That left the door open for Namibia to sneak through if they could beat hosts Madagascar by 53 points in Antananarivo and an 89-10 success saw Namibia join Zimbabwe and Kenya on 10 points, but Namibia

claimed the title by virtue of having a superior points difference and took their place alongside New Zealand, Argentina, Tonga and Georgia in Pool C. Zimbabwe fell into the Repechage, at Kenya's expense, where they lost to Russia.

Georgia's Pool C place was secured by a 22-9 defeat of Romania in Tbilisi in front of 27,000 supporters. By finishing in the top two places in the European Nations Cup — ahead of Russia, Spain, Portugal and Belgium — both sides knew their passage to Rugby World Cup 2015 was safe and the result of their clash determined in which pool they would compete at England 2015. The foundation for victory was a stellar forward display which saw Georgia advance to the Millennium Stadium, where their Rugby World Cup 2015 campaign will open against New Zealand. The Lelos came close to upsetting Scotland in the 2011 Tournament and even the All Blacks will be wary of facing their formidable forwards.

Romania's defeat saw them take the Europe 2 place in Pool D, which also comprises France, Ireland, Italy and Canada. This continued the Oaks' proud record of participation in every edition of the Rugby World Cup. Invited to the inaugural Tournament in 1987, they have earned qualification ever since.

Canada, likewise, maintained their record of appearing at every edition of the Tournament. They did so by beating neighbours the United States.

The Canucks became the first qualifiers from the global qualification process by beating the US Eagles 40-20 on aggregate, although they could only manage a 13-11 victory in the second leg in Toronto after a 27-9 win in the USA and head coach Kieran Crowley admitted: "It was ugly but it was a win."

The pursuit of a place in the knockout stages begins when the Tournament starts on September 18 but simply being involved represents success for those that have had to earn their place the hard way.

POOL A

September 18	20:00	Twickenham, London
England		**Fiji**

September 20	14:30	Millennium Stadium, Cardiff
Wales		**Uruguay**

September 23	16:45	Millennium Stadium, Cardiff
Australia		**Fiji**

September 26	20:00	Twickenham, London
England		**Wales**

September 27	12:00	Villa Park, Birmingham
Australia		**Uruguay**

October 1	16:45	Millennium Stadium, Cardiff
Wales		**Fiji**

October 3	20:00	Twickenham, London
England		**Australia**

October 6	20:00	Stadium MK, Milton Keynes
Fiji		**Uruguay**

October 10	16:45	Twickenham, London
Australia		**Wales**

October 10	20:00	Manchester City Stadium
England		**Uruguay**

FINAL POOL A TABLE

Pos	Team	P	W	L	D	PF	PA	Pts
A1								
A2								
A3								
A4								
A5								

POOL B

September 19	16:45	Brighton Community Stadium
South Africa		**Japan**

September 20	12:00	Brighton Community Stadium
Samoa		**United States**

September 23	14:30	Kingsholm, Gloucester
Scotland		**Japan**

September 26	16:45	Villa Park, Birmingham
South Africa		**Samoa**

September 27	14:30	Elland Road, Leeds
Scotland		**United States**

October 3	14:30	Stadium MK, Milton Keynes
Samoa		**Japan**

October 3	16:45	St James' Park, Newcastle
South Africa		**Scotland**

October 7	16:45	Olympic Stadium, London
South Africa		**United States**

October 10	14:30	St James' Park, Newcastle
Samoa		**Scotland**

October 11	20:00	Kingsholm, Gloucester
United States		**Japan**

FINAL POOL B TABLE

Pos	Team	P	W	L	D	PF	PA	Pts
B1								
B2								
B3								
B4								
B5								

QUARTER-FINALS

QF1	16:00	Twickenham, London
B1		A2

QF2	20:00	Millennium Stadium, Cardiff
C1		D2

QF3	13:00	Millennium Stadium, Cardiff
D1		C2

QF4	16:00	Twickenham, London
A1		B2

SEMI-FINALS

SF1	16:00	Twickenham, London
Winner QF1		Winner QF2

SF2	16:00	Twickenham, London
Winner QF3		Winner QF4

BRONZE FINAL

	20:00	Olympic Stadium, London
Runner-up SF1		Runner-up SF2

POOL C

September 19	12:00	Kingsholm, Gloucester
Tonga		**Georgia**

September 20	16:45	Wembley Stadium, London
New Zealand		**Argentina**

September 24	20:00	Olympic Stadium, London
New Zealand		**Namibia**

September 25	16:45	Kingsholm, Gloucester
Argentina		**Georgia**

September 29	16:45	Sandy Park, Exeter
Tonga		**Namibia**

October 2	20:00	Millennium Stadium, Cardiff
New Zealand		**Georgia**

October 4	14:30	Leicester City Stadium
Argentina		**Tonga**

October 7	20:00	Sandy Park, Exeter
Namibia		**Georgia**

October 9	20:00	St James' Park, Newcastle
New Zealand		**Tonga**

October 11	12:00	Leicester City Stadium
Argentina		**Namibia**

FINAL POOL C TABLE

Pos	Team	P	W	L	D	PF	PA	Pts
C1								
C2								
C3								
C4								
C5								

POOL D

September 19	14:30	Millennium Stadium, Cardiff
Ireland		**Canada**

September 19	20:00	Twickenham, London
France		**Italy**

September 23	20:00	Olympic Stadium, London
France		**Romania**

September 26	14:30	Elland Road, Leeds
Italy		**Canada**

September 27	16:45	Wembley Stadium, London
Ireland		**Romania**

October 1	20:00	Stadium MK, Milton Keynes
France		**Canada**

October 4	16:45	Olympic Stadium, London
Ireland		**Italy**

October 6	16:45	Leicester City Stadium
Canada		**Romania**

October 11	14:30	Sandy Park, Exeter
Italy		**Romania**

October 11	16:45	Millennium Stadium, Cardiff
France		**Ireland**

FINAL POOL D TABLE

Pos	Team	P	W	L	D	PF	PA	Pts
D1								
D2								
D3								
D4								
D5								

RUGBY WORLD CUP 2015 FINAL

	16:00		Twickenham, London	
Winner SF1				Winner SF2

RUGBY WORLD CUP 2015 CHAMPIONS

All kick-offs listed in local time.

World Rugby Rankings

WORLD RUGBY™

There have been few signs of New Zealand's dominance waning since winning Rugby World Cup 2011 on home turf in Auckland, and the All Blacks' superiority is reflected in their proud position at number one in the World Rugby Rankings as they prepare to defend their cherished crown.

HOW THEY WORK

The World Rugby Rankings, introduced in 2003, is a system used to rank the world's international teams based on their results, with all teams given a rating between 0 and 100.

The rankings are based on a points-exchange system in which sides take or gain points off each other depending on the result of a match. The points gained or lost in a match depend on the relative strengths of each team and the margin of defeat or victory with an allowance made for teams who have home advantage.

Due to the importance of the event, points are doubled for Rugby World Cup matches.

Challengers South Africa

Steve Hansen's men lost only two of their next 42 matches following the Rugby World Cup 2011 Final victory over France which ended the nation's 24-year wait for glory.

The All Blacks, who won the inaugural Tournament in 1987, lost to England at Twickenham in December 2012, seeing a 20-match unbeaten streak end. They were beaten again in October 2014 when they were edged out 27-25 by fellow two-time world champions South Africa. That ended a 23-match run without a defeat, but the loss in Johannesburg might have been forecast as the All Blacks had been denied a record 18th successive win by Australia in the opening game of the Rugby Championship two months earlier.

Everyone is trying to knock the reigning champions from their pedestal after five years as the world's number one nation, with the Springboks being their closest challengers.

Ireland led the European challenge at the end of 2014 and occupied third place in the rankings but the seedings for Rugby World Cup 2015 were decided at the end of the 2012, when Australia were in third place. They had slipped to fifth by the end of 2014 following a European autumn tour in which they managed to win only one of their four matches.

That saw them slip below England and only one place above Wales to highlight the fact that Pool A is undoubtedly the 'Pool of Death' at Rugby World Cup 2015, featuring three of the best six teams in the world, based on the rankings at the end of 2014. Wales dropped into the third pot of seeds in late 2012 but have been on the rise since then.

It could also be tight to determine who advances from Pool B, with South Africa favourites and third seeds Scotland now ranked higher than second seeds Samoa.

Scotland had slumped in the rankings ahead of the Rugby World Cup 2015 draw, before climbing back above Argentina. Pool B also includes Asian Five Nations champions Japan, who are ranked 11th, and the United States, who are ranked in 16th place.

Ninth-ranked Argentina are second seeds in Pool C behind New Zealand, with Tonga four ranking places behind them and seeking to upset the South Americans in the Tournament.

Nineteen of the world's top 20 nations are represented at England 2015 with the exception being Namibia, who are ranked 23rd in the world, below Russia, Spain and Portugal. They squeezed through to the Tournament in qualifying ahead of Zimbabwe and Kenya. Namibia also play the All Blacks, Argentina, Tonga and Georgia, whose powerful pack are largely responsible for their ranking of 15th.

France have dropped to seventh and below Ireland ahead of their Pool D meeting, with 14th-ranked Italy also in the mix. Romania and Canada, who are ranked 17th and 18th, respectively, complete the pool.

New Zealand have cemented their place as the world's best team since regaining the Webb Ellis Cup four years ago

WORLD RUGBY RANKINGS – TOP 50

Pos	Team	Points	Pos	Team	Points	Pos	Team	Points
1	**New Zealand**	**93.70**	18	Canada	66.83	35	Brazil	51.31
2	South Africa	88.23	19	Russia	64.12	36	Czech Republic	51.25
3	Ireland	85.48	20	Uruguay	63.58	37	Morocco	51.18
4	England	84.85	21	Spain	60.65	38	Tunisia	49.89
5	Australia	82.95	22	Portugal	58.56	39	Paraguay	49.74
6	Wales	81.64	23	Namibia	58.27	40	Kazakhstan	48.91
7	France	79.66	24	Korea	57.22	41	Malta	48.74
8	Scotland	78.78	25	Germany	56.32	42	Senegal	48.69
9	Argentina	78.23	26	Zimbabwe	55.83	43	Madagascar	47.69
10	Samoa	75.39	27	Hong Kong	55.79	44	Lithuania	47.65
11	Japan	74.70	28	Moldova	55.38	45	Switzerland	47.22
12	Fiji	74.57	29	Chile	54.54	46	Cook Islands	47.11
13	Tonga	74.12	30	Belgium	54.50	47	Cote d'Ivoire	47.08
14	Italy	71.19	31	Kenya	53.25	48	Sri Lanka	46.95
15	Georgia	70.76	32	Ukraine	52.33	49	Croatia	46.47
16	USA	67.61	33	Netherlands	52.25	50	Colombia	46.37
17	Romania	67.38	34	Poland	51.33		as of December 31, 2014	

Above: Defending Rugby World Cup champions New Zealand will again be the team to beat in 2015

Far left: Wales, semi-finalists in 2011, have been handed a tough task, drawn in the same pool as Australia and England

Left: France will be hoping to go one better at Rugby World Cup 2015 than in 1987, 1999 and 2011 when they were runners-up

Right: Much will be expected of hosts England, captained by Chris Robshaw, who will have the advantage of playing three of their four pool matches on familiar territory at Twickenham

MEET THE TEAMS

Reigning champions New Zealand and three other previous winners – Australia, South Africa and England – are among 20 nations that will contest Rugby World Cup 2015. The very best of northern and southern hemispheres will collide in eagerly-anticipated fashion during six weeks of thrills, spills and high drama when the Game's biggest names take centre stage, while new stars will also emerge into the Game's brightest and most coveted spotlight as the Rugby world awaits another glittering showpiece.

Australia

Australia have a proud Rugby World Cup record, but it is hard to know what shape the squad will be in as they look to lift the Webb Ellis Cup for a third time. Their 2014 Rugby Championship was disappointing but the Wallabies have a habit of coming into their own at Rugby World Cups and again expect to be leading contenders.

Australia have matched their great southern hemisphere rivals New Zealand and South Africa by winning the Webb Ellis Cup on two occasions, but both successes came in the 1990s. Since then, the Wallabies have been competitive but have failed to take the final step.

It would be unwise to rule the Rugby World Cup 1991 and 1999 champions out of contention, given their ability to produce some of the Game's finest talent, most notably quick-thinking playmakers and dynamic strike runners capable of changing the course of a match. But an old Achilles heel, the scrum, continues to be exposed, while fortune has not smiled on their draw, with England and Wales plotting to prevent Australia reaching the knockout stages for the first time.

Given their playing numbers and their public's preference for other codes, Australia punch above their weight in continuing to be counted among Rugby's superpowers. It was their triumph at Rugby World Cup 1991 which secured a seat at the top table, a seat they show no sign of relinquishing.

Four years earlier they were semi-finalists in a Rugby World Cup they co-hosted with New Zealand and, while fancied by some to become champions, they went out in a 30-24 defeat to France. Much of the groundwork for 1991 had been laid, though, with David Campese, Michael Lynagh and Nick Farr-Jones among those emerging as world-class.

During the 1980s, the Wallabies had earned their reputation as the Game's innovators, led by the brilliance of Mark Ella, who redefined the role of fly-half. By 1991 they had built a pack capable of standing toe to toe with all opponents, based around the spine of Phil Kearns, John Eales and Willie Ofahengaue. Ella may have gone, but in Lynagh they had the shrewdest of Generals with the temperament to match. Outside

Australia

www.rugby.com.au

PLAYING STRIP Gold shirts with green trim, green shorts, green socks

FORM SINCE RUGBY WORLD CUP 2011

Played:	45
Won:	23
Lost:	20
Drawn:	2
Winning percentage:	53.3%
Points for:	985
Points against:	1,041
Points scored per match:	21.9
Points conceded per match:	23.1
Biggest victory:	54-17 v Argentina at Gigante de Arroyito on October 5, 2013
Heaviest defeat:	33-6 v France at Stade de France on November 10, 2012
World Rugby Ranking (at Jan 2015)	5

RUGBY WORLD CUP PERFORMANCES

1987	Semi-finals
1991	WORLD CHAMPIONS
1995	Quarter-finals
1999	WORLD CHAMPIONS
2003	Runners-up
2007	Quarter-finals
2011	Semi-finals

COACH

MICHAEL CHEIKA

Cheika stepped up to the national team, though remaining the NSW Waratahs coach, soon after Ewen McKenzie resigned in October 2014. McKenzie's reign ended after a year of average results. Cheika has an impressive track record at club level, guiding Leinster to their first European Cup crown in 2009 and the Waratahs to the 2014 Super Rugby title in only his second season in charge. A fiery character who is unafraid to make his opinions known, Cheika was seen as the ideal candidate to steer the Wallabies back on track.

His Rugby philosophy is to field a physical pack while allowing his backs the freedom to express themselves.

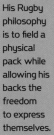

Lynagh, stood the centre partnership of Tim Horan and Jason Little, possibly the greatest midfield pairing the Game has seen. England were defeated 12-6 in the Twickenham Final and Australia had their finest hour.

Many of the heroes from 1991 remained for the third Rugby World Cup in South Africa, but the magic touch had deserted them in a disappointing Tournament that ended with a 25-22 defeat by England in the quarter-finals, having already been well beaten by the hosts in the pool stages.

There was no Campese, Lynagh or Ofahengaue in 1999, but Australia

STAR PLAYER

MICHAEL HOOPER

Position:	Flanker
Born:	October 29, 1991
	Collaroy, New South Wales, Australia
Club:	Waratahs (Aus)
Height:	1.83m (6ft)
Weight:	101kg (15st 13lb)
Caps:	42
Points:	35 (7t)

From the moment he made his debut against Scotland in 2012, it was clear Michael Hooper had a bright Test future. Injury resulted in the Waratahs flanker being given the Wallabies captaincy and he responded by announcing his arrival as a world-class openside, possibly the best in his position. A poacher in the classic Australian mould, Hooper's strength over the ball and intuition for the timing of his steals set him apart. Despite often being the smallest forward on the pitch, he is a marauding ball-carrier who knows how to pick the right line and he is still only 23.

Australia have won the Rugby World Cup twice

demolished at the scrum in what has become a recurring weakness.

Ireland were provided with their greatest Rugby World Cup victory in 2011 when they defeated Australia 15-6 in Auckland, but the Wallabies were still able to progress to the quarter-finals. A brutal contest saw the vastly-experienced South Africa toppled 11-9, but Australia had emptied the tanks and they lost 20-6 to New Zealand in the semi-finals.

Though not the force of old, the Wallabies have too much firepower to be written off this time. Openside and captain Michael Hooper is among the finest forwards in the Game, while Israel Folau, Will Genia and Quade Cooper have the wit to unlock any defence.

Australia's vulnerabilities are all too obvious, however, with opponents knowing the value of pounding away at their scrum and against a tight five inferior to that of their biggest rivals. There is also the sense that the once-great innovators of the Game, who produce runners to match the All Blacks, have lost their identity to some extent. But come Rugby World Cup 2015, it would surprise nobody if a combination of rugby intelligence and Australian tenacity sweeps them to the Twickenham Final.

PLAYERS TO WATCH

1. STEPHEN MOORE
Age: 32; *Position:* Hooker; *Club:* Brumbies (Aus); *Caps:* 92; *Points:* 25 (5t)

2. ISRAEL FOLAU
Age: 26; *Position:* Full-back; *Club:* Waratahs (Aus); *Caps:* 29; *Points:* 85 (17t)

3. ADAM ASHLEY-COOPER
Age: 31; *Position:* Centre/wing; *Club:* Waratahs (Aus); *Caps:* 104; *Points:* 150 (30t)

4. BERNARD FOLEY
Age: 25; *Position:* Fly-half; *Club:* Waratahs (Aus); *Caps:* 18; *Points:* 156 (4t, 26c, 27p, 1dg)

5. WILL GENIA
Age: 27; *Position:* Scrum-half; *Club:* Reds (Aus); *Caps:* 58; *Points:* 40 (8t)

remained as potent as ever with Joe Roff, Stephen Larkham and Ben Tune offering the dynamism that, by now, had become synonymous with the Wallabies. Their route to the Final accounted for Ireland, Wales and South Africa, but the showpiece itself proved one of their easiest assignments as they swept aside France 35-12.

Australia were sole hosts in 2003, but they were unable to become the first team to defend the Webb Ellis Cup, something yet to be achieved by any team. England avenged their defeat in the 1991 Final when a drop-goal from Jonny Wilkinson secured a 20-17 victory in extra-time. The Wallabies had disposed of New Zealand in the semi-finals but, in truth, England should have emerged more convincing winners from the Sydney showpiece.

The rivalry continued into 2007 and once again the supremacy of the England pack paved the way for victory as Stirling Mortlock's Wallabies were edged out 12-10 in Marseille. The quarter-final exit proved harrowing for Australia's front row, who were

England

England have come a long way since their below-par performance at Rugby World Cup 2011. Stuart Lancaster has steadily rebuilt the squad based on foundations of youthful exuberance, discipline and skill. Their constant improvement under the former schoolteacher has fans dreaming of a Rugby World Cup win on home soil.

When Martin Johnson lifted the Webb Ellis Cup in a blaze of glory in 2003, many hoped it would be the start of a dynasty but England have found it difficult to replicate that achievement.

As big players retired, injuries mounted and Sir Clive Woodward moved on to pastures new, England lost the essence of what made them the best side in the world after twice going out at the quarter-final stage, once in the semi-finals and finishing runners-up in previous Rugby World Cups.

Prior to 2003 it was a case of 'so near but yet so far' for England, with the inaugural 1987 Tournament seeing them lose 16-3 to Wales in the quarter-finals. Four years later, on home soil, the English reached the Final under Geoff Cooke's stewardship but fell just short of glory, losing the showpiece at Twickenham 12-6 to Australia. In South Africa in 1995, England managed to get some revenge for that defeat, beating the Wallabies 25-22 in the quarter-finals, before New Zealand – and the imperious Jonah Lomu – comprehensively dumped them out in the semis with a 45-29 thrashing.

Back in the northern hemisphere, under Woodward's leadership, England suffered more Rugby World Cup disappointment in 1999 when they were left licking their wounds after being beaten 44-21 by a powerful Springboks display in the quarter-finals. However, the emergence of Jonny Wilkinson on the global stage was a positive to take from the Tournament as Woodward began fashioning the nucleus of a side that would dominate in 2003.

With Wilkinson's unerring accuracy with the boot behind a formidable pack, led by Johnson, they enjoyed a fine run of form – beating both New Zealand and Australia in their own backyards – and arrived in Australia as favourites to lift the Webb Ellis Cup. This was the second Rugby World Cup in the professional era and Woodward was meticulous in his preparations which helped to ensure they efficiently dealt with all put before them in the pool stage. After trickier tests in the knockout rounds against Wales and France respectively, England secured a rematch of the 1991 Final, this time on Australian soil. The rest is history as Wilkinson's last-gasp drop goal sealed a 20-17 victory in extra-time.

Far from building on that flawless showing in 2003, England's empire

COACH

STUART LANCASTER

The former Leeds Carnegie director of Rugby has steadied the ship after a turbulent few years. Lancaster, who is supported in the coaching set-up by former internationals Andy Farrell, Graham Rowntree and Mike Catt, has enjoyed a number of impressive results since taking over in 2011. His meticulous approach has overseen England's defence becoming one of the meanest in the northern hemisphere, while there have been signs of a more expansive game recently, which bodes well for the future. There have been criticisms of his frequent use of substitutions, but that could pay dividends if it develops a host of battle-hardened players to choose from.

England Rugby

England
www.rfu.com

PLAYING STRIP White shirts, white shorts, black socks

FORM SINCE RUGBY WORLD CUP 2011

Played:	34
Won:	20
Lost:	13
Drawn:	1
Winning percentage:	60.29%
Points for:	823
Points against:	604
Points scored per match:	24.2
Points conceded per match:	17.8
Biggest victory:	54-12 v Fiji
at Twickenham on November 10, 2012	
Heaviest defeat:	30-3 v Wales
at Millennium Stadium on March 16, 2013	
World Rugby Ranking (at Jan 2015)	4

RUGBY WORLD CUP PERFORMANCES

1987	Quarter-finals
1991	Runners-up
1995	Semi-finals
1999	Quarter-finals
2003	WORLD CHAMPIONS
2007	Runners-up
2011	Quarter-finals

STAR PLAYER

MIKE BROWN

Position:..Full-back
Born:..September 4, 1985
	Southampton, England
Club:..Harlequins (Eng)
Height:..1.83m (6ft)
Weight:..89kg (196lb)
Caps:..33
Points:..30 (6t)

The Harlequins full-back spent a rather subdued 2013 Six Nations stuck out on the wing, but he exploded into life playing at 15 in 2014 to become England's key man. His reliability under the high ball and elusive running have been delighting the Twickenham Stoop crowd for years, but thanks to specialist sprint training with former Scottish hurdles champion Margot Wells, he has found extra pace to translate that to the international stage. There is a fiery side to Brown, who is nicknamed 'Mr Angry' by his Quins team-mates, which drives him to never take a backward step.

of Ben Foden and finishing of Chris Ashton, Johnson delivered the first Six Nations title for eight years only months before the global showpiece. But Johnson's side bowed out at the quarter-finals – their worst performance in a Rugby World Cup since 1999 – with a lacklustre 19-12 defeat to France and were besieged by unsavoury off-field controversies throughout their time in New Zealand.

It was a disappointing farewell to the last remaining 2003 stalwarts in Wilkinson, Lewis Moody and Mike Tindall, but it may just prove to be the cleansing experience that finally allows England to prosper again.

With all links to the 2003 success severed after Johnson's resignation, Stuart Lancaster immediately looked to usher in a new era as head coach. He has brought in exciting young stars such as Owen Farrell and Joe Launchbury, while Chris Robshaw has led his impressive pack with an authority that belies his years.

These young guns led England to a shock 38-21 victory over world champions New Zealand in 2012 and subsequent home victories over Rugby World Cup 2015 Pool A opponents Wales and Australia have fans excited about what Lancaster's side are capable of.

started to crumble as the rest of the northern hemisphere caught up in the Six Nations leading up to Rugby World Cup 2007.

During the early stages in France, it looked set to be a painful experience for England as they were beaten 36-0 in the pool match by South Africa. Against all the odds, though, England, now led by Brian Ashton, stunned pundits and fans alike to fight back and reach the Final for the third time – only to be beaten 15-6 by South Africa again.

In 2011 it had seemed like Johnson himself, who took over the coaching reins from Ashton, was preparing a side capable of challenging for the Webb Ellis Cup again, before things turned sour in New Zealand.

Spearheaded by the direct running

England have been steadily rebuilt under the stewardship of Stuart Lancaster

PLAYERS TO WATCH

1. CHRIS ROBSHAW
Age: 29; *Position:* back row; *Club:* Harlequins (Eng); *Caps:* 32; *Points:* 10 (2t)

2. OWEN FARRELL
Age: 23; *Position:* fly-half; *Club:* Saracens (Eng); *Caps:* 29; *Points:* 290 (2t, 35c, 69pg, 1dg)

3. JOE LAUNCHBURY
Age: 24; *Position:* lock; *Club:* London Wasps (Eng); *Caps:* 22; *Points:* 10 (2t)

4. BILLY VUNIPOLA
Age: 22; *Position:* back row; *Club:* Saracens (Eng); *Caps:* 12; *Points:* 5 (1t)

5. BEN YOUNGS
Age: 25; *Position:* scrum-half; *Club:* Leicester (Eng); *Caps:* 44; *Points:* 30 (6t)

Wales

Wales reached their first semi-final since the inaugural 1987 competition at Rugby World Cup 2011, then won a second Six Nations Grand Slam of coach Warren Gatland's reign five months later before successfully defending the title in 2013. They remain one of the most dangerous teams in world Rugby.

Wales
www.wru.co.uk

PLAYING STRIP Red shirts, red shorts, red socks

FORM SINCE RUGBY WORLD CUP 2011

Played:	36
Won:	18
Lost:	18
Drawn:	0
Winning percentage:	50%
Points for:	762
Points against:	682
Points scored per match:	21.2
Points conceded per match:	18.9
Biggest victory:	51-3 v Scotland at Millennium Stadium on March 15, 2014
Heaviest defeats:	33-10 v New Zealand at Millennium Stadium on Nov 24, 2012
	26-3 v Ireland at Aviva Stadium on February 8, 2014
World Rugby Ranking (at Jan 2015)	6

RUGBY WORLD CUP PERFORMANCES

1987	Semi-finals
1991	Pool stages
1995	Pool stages
1999	Quarter-finals
2003	Quarter-finals
2007	Pool stages
2011	Semi-finals

Wales' Rugby World Cup performances have been something of a mixed bag, with highs and lows seemingly going hand in hand from the first Tournament 28 years ago all the way through to Rugby World Cup 2011 in New Zealand.

Their first Rugby World Cup match in 1987 was against familiar foes Ireland in Wellington and they made a winning start to the inaugural Tournament, earning a 13-6 victory in what was expected to be the toughest contest in a pool that also included Tonga and Canada. And so it proved, as Wales journeyed two hours north to Palmerston North, where they defeated Tonga 29-16, before heading to the tip of New Zealand's South Island and Invercargill, where they eased to a 40-9 success against Canada as wing Ieuan Evans scored four tries.

Arch-rivals England were Wales' quarter-final opponents across the Tasman Sea in Brisbane and a scrappy encounter produced a 16-3 win. Wales then faced the testing prospect of a last-four appointment with co-hosts and Tournament favourites New Zealand, and the All Blacks powered home 49-6 as their opponents also had Huw Richards sent off. Wales, though, did gain some consolation when Paul Thorburn's last-gasp kick in Rotorua saw them edge past Australia 22-21 to finish third.

Four years later, Wales had what appeared to be a considerable advantage of playing their three pool matches on home soil at Cardiff Arms Park, but their campaign plunged into a nightmare as they were stunned 16-13 by Western Samoa. It meant they had to beat Argentina three days later, which they did 16-7, but eventual finalists Australia proved too strong, romping home 38-3 as Wallaby legends David Campese, Tim Horan and Michael Lynagh all scored tries. The ignominy of going out at the pool phase was felt long and hard in Wales, but life was not about to get any easier four years later in South Africa, where a testing pool saw them drawn alongside New Zealand, Ireland and Japan.

Japan were duly defeated 57-10 in Bloemfontein, where Gareth Thomas scored three tries, but a 34-9 loss to New Zealand meant Wales had to beat Ireland at Johannesburg's Ellis Park in their quest for a quarter-final place. An agonising 24-23 loss, though,

COACH

WARREN GATLAND

New Zealander Warren Gatland took the Wales hot-seat in early 2008, and immediately inspired a Grand Slam-winning campaign. Assisted by his experienced coaching lieutenants Rob Howley, Shaun Edwards, Robin McBryde and Neil Jenkins, Gatland has won rave reviews for his meticulous attention to detail and continuing to grow Wales' state-of-the-art training facilities at their Vale of Glamorgan base. He has also not been afraid to give young players a chance at Test level alongside established names and, on their day, Wales remain a match for any team, anywhere.

STAR PLAYER

LEIGH HALFPENNY

Position:...Full-back
Born:..........December 22, 1988, Gorseinon, Wales
Club:...Toulon (Fra)
Height:.......................................1.78m (5ft 10in)
Weight:...88kg (194lb)
Caps:..55
Points:.............................422 (12t, 31c, 100p)

Leigh Halfpenny might be relatively small compared with some of Rugby's modern-day giants, but his stature has grown and grown since he made his Wales debut as a 19-year-old in 2008. He gained selection for the following year's British and Irish Lions tour to South Africa, and then starred at Rugby World Cup 2011 before his career enjoyed lift-off. He inspired Wales' 2012 Six Nations Grand Slam triumph, and was named player of the tournament during a successful title defence 12 months later. When the Lions toured Australia that summer, Halfpenny's form and goal-kicking saw him claim a Test series record 49 points and be named player of the series.

emphatically ended Wales' interest.

By the time Wales arrived in Australia for Rugby World Cup 2003, they were under the coaching direction of Steve Hansen, who succeeded his fellow New Zealander Graham Henry, and there was an invigorating attacking approach that surfaced during an epic encounter against the All Blacks. Wales lost 53-37 in Sydney, but they scored four tries to New Zealand's five, and set up a mouth-watering quarter-final against England following earlier victories over Canada, Tonga and Italy. Despite Wales leading the eventual world champions at half-time, they eventually succumbed 28-17 and were left to reflect on what might have been.

An early exit at Rugby World Cup 2007 – Wales were knocked out by Fiji in Nantes following an attacking spectacular – and Warren Gatland was soon installed as head coach. By the time Wales arrived at Rugby World Cup 2011, they had won a Six Nations Grand Slam and went on to enjoy an outstanding campaign, beating Ireland in the quarter-finals before suffering an agonising 9-8 semi-final loss to France after skipper Sam Warburton was sent off midway through the first half.

Wales then successfully defended the Six Nations title in 2013, and they will be very much a team to watch at Rugby World Cup 2015, even though a quarter-final place would be achieved the hard way as England and Australia are in the same pool.

consigned them to an early flight home for the second successive Rugby World Cup campaign and another lengthy post mortem.

As it had done eight years earlier, Wales' Rugby World Cup 1999 pool also featured Samoa and Argentina. Incredibly, Samoa beat Wales in Cardiff again, this time enjoying a 38-31 success, but the men in red had already won their opening two matches against Argentina and Japan, which booked a quarter-final berth for the first time since 1987. Eventual Tournament winners Australia proved too strong in the last eight, though, as they

PLAYERS TO WATCH

1. GEORGE NORTH
Age: 23; *Position:* wing; *Club:* Northampton (Eng); *Caps:* 45; *Points:* 95 (19t)

2. SAM WARBURTON
Age: 26; *Position:* flanker; *Club:* Cardiff Blues (Wal); *Caps:* 49; *Points:* 15 (3t)

3. ALUN WYN JONES
Age: 29; *Position:* lock; *Club:* Ospreys (Wal); *Caps:* 84; *Points:* 40 (8t)

4. MIKE PHILLIPS
Age: 32; *Position:* scrum-half; *Club:* Racing Métro (Fra); *Caps:* 90; *Points:* 45 (9t)

5. TAULUPE FALETAU
Age: 24; *Position:* number 8; *Club:* Newport Gwent Dragons (Wal); *Caps:* 40; *Points:* 20 (4t)

Semi-finalists in 2011, Wales face a tough task to get out of their pool this time

Fiji

A fan favourite of world Rugby, Fiji can produce the spectacular and sublime one moment but play like a team of strangers the next. Reaching the Rugby World Cup 2015 knockout phase could be beyond the current crop given they share a pool with England, Wales and Australia but, as always, Fiji could cause an upset or two.

For all their flamboyance, finesse and power, Fiji have never been able to replicate their Sevens success in 15-a-side Rugby. It is in the shorter format that the Flying Fijians have consistently left their mark on the world stage and, while two Rugby World Cup quarter-finals are not to be sniffed at,

they should boast a better record in the traditional game.

A quarter-final finish in the inaugural Rugby World Cup in New Zealand in 1987 pointed to a bright future for Fijian Rugby but, rather than build on that promise after losing to eventual runners-up France, the Fijians have yet to better that performance since then.

One try in three pool matches saw them suffer an early exit from RWC 1991 and it got even worse four years later when they did not qualify for Rugby World Cup 1995 in South Africa.

An unfortunate 28-19 defeat in their Rugby World Cup 1999 pool match against France cost Fiji a place in the quarter-finals, but they only had themselves to blame for a first-round exit at Rugby World Cup 2003 in Australia.

Fiji secured their second quarter-final appearance at Rugby World Cup 2007 thanks to a 38-34 victory over Wales – arguably their greatest ever Rugby World Cup performance – and gave a good account of themselves before going down 37-20 to eventual winners South Africa in the last eight.

A 27-7 defeat to rivals Samoa saw Fiji slump to another early exit when New Zealand hosted Rugby World Cup 2011 but, after falling five places to 16th in the World Rugby Rankings in the aftermath, Fiji have been on an upward trend since. They finished runners-up to Samoa in the 2012 Pacific Nations Cup, and went one better to win the 2013 title and climb back up

COACH

JOHN McKEE

New Zealander John McKee's appointment as Fiji coach in May 2014 certainly had a 'right place, right time' feel to it. The then FRU's High Performance Unit general manager jumped at the chance to succeed Inoke Male after the former Fiji number 8 was given his marching orders at the start of the year. Critics would suggest that McKee's behind-the-scenes stints with Tonga and Australia's Under-20 side are scant preparation for the cut-throat nature of life as an international head coach but he has taken to the task with aplomb and, slowly but surely, is winning over the doubters.

Fiji
www.fijirugby.com

PLAYING STRIP White shirts with black trim, black shorts, black and white striped socks

FORM SINCE RUGBY WORLD CUP 2011

Played:	22
Won:	13
Lost:	9
Drawn:	0
Winning percentage:	59.1%
Points for:	615
Points against:	484
Points scored per match:	27.95
Points conceded per match:	22.00
Biggest victory:	108-6 v Cook Islands in Suva on June 28, 2014
Heaviest defeat:	54-12 v England at Twickenham on November 10, 2012
World Rugby Ranking (at Jan 2015):	12

RUGBY WORLD CUP PERFORMANCES

1987	Quarter-finals
1991	Pool stages
1995	Did not qualify
1999	Quarter-final play-offs
2003	Pool stages
2007	Quarter-finals
2011	Pool stages

to 11th in the rankings. John McKee's appointment as coach in May 2014 surprised many but, while Fiji could not retain their Pacific Nations Cup crown in the revamped 2014 competition, a 45-17 defeat of Tonga suggests they remain on the right path. More impressively, Fiji pulled off an encouraging 25-14 victory over Italy in June last year, courtesy of a 13-point match haul from Nemani Nadolo, and then secured qualification for Rugby World Cup 2015 with a 17-try, 108-6 defeat of the Cook Islands.

Fiji have the honour of facing hosts England in the opening match of

STAR PLAYER

NEMANI NADOLO

Position:..................................Centre/wing
Born:....................January 31, 1988, Sigatoka, Fiji
Club:...............................Crusaders (NZL))
Height:..............................1.96m (6ft 5in)
Weight:.........................125kg (275lb)
Caps:..18
Points:.........................123 (14t, 13c, 9p)

A cousin of former Australia wing Lote Tuqiri, Nemani Nadolo's imposing frame and turn of pace has led some to compare him with All Black great Jonah Lomu. Nadolo joined New Zealand franchise the Crusaders in 2014 after stints playing club Rugby in Australia, France, England and Japan. Twelve tries in 14 appearances guided the Crusaders to within a whisker of the Super Rugby title and his semi-final display against the Sharks was one of the outstanding performances of the season. He is equally prolific on the international stage and his incisive runs will provide much of Fiji's attacking threat.

told Fiji Rugby Union's official website. "One of them will get knocked out. Personally, I think we should have a different attitude to Rugby World Cup this time. We are not going there to win it, so let's go there to put bums on seats. Let's spread the message of Fiji Rugby and Pacific Islands Rugby."

While Little may no longer be on hand to galvanise the national team, there is a plethora of talent at McKee's disposal that, if harnessed in the right way, could achieve great things. Crusaders winger Nadolo finished the 2014 Super Rugby season as joint-top try-scorer with 12 touchdowns and his man-of-the-match display against the Sharks in the semi-finals was one of the individual performances of the season. Asaeli Tikoirotuma helped the Chiefs to back-to-back Super Rugby titles in 2012 and 2013 before joining national team captain Akapusi Qera in the northern hemisphere after agreeing a two-year deal at English side Harlequins. Qera plies his trade in the Top 14 with Montpellier and McKee will need this talented triumvirate to perform to the best of their considerable abilities if Fiji are to achieve the unlikely and avoid an early exit for a second Rugby World Cup in succession.

Fiji's best Rugby World Cup moment came when they beat Wales in 2007

Rugby World Cup 2015 on September 18 and while Stuart Lancaster's side will be favourites to come out on top, a solid performance will be required in order to gather some much-needed momentum ahead of tricky remaining Pool A fixtures. It does not get any easier for the Fijians, though, as they follow up the Twickenham encounter with Millennium Stadium battles against Wales and Australia before concluding their pool action against Uruguay in Milton Keynes.

Fiji's record appearance holder and points scorer Nicky Little believes that, given they are not expected to progress from their pool, Fiji should play without fear and try to entertain the spectators as well as the global audience. "This is the Pool of Death for the big boys," he

PLAYERS TO WATCH

1. ASAELI TIKOIROTUMA
Age: 29; *Position:* wing; *Club:* Harlequins (Eng); *Caps:* 9; *Points:* 10 (2t)

2. AKAPUSI QERA
Age: 31; *Position:* flanker; *Club:* Montpellier (Fra); *Caps:* 42; *Points:* 35 (7t)

3. METUISELA TALEBULA
Age: 24; *Position:* full-back; *Club:* Bordeaux-Bègles (Fra); *Caps:* 13; *Points:* 43 (7t, 1c, 1p, 1dg)

4. VERENIKI GONEVA
Age: 31; *Position:* centre/wing; *Club:* Leicester (Eng); *Caps:* 31; *Points:* 70 (14t)

5. NIKOLA MATAWALU
Age: 26; *Position:* scrum-half; *Club:* Glasgow (Sco); *Caps:* 21; *Points:* 25 (5t)

Uruguay

Uruguay have, historically, been one of the strongest nations in South America, but it has been 12 years since Los Teros have made it to a Rugby World Cup. Their return is welcome, as they play with fervour and passion, while Uruguay's power in the scrum gives them hope in any contest.

URU

Uruguay
www.uru.org.uy

PLAYING STRIP Light blue shirts, black shorts, black socks

FORM SINCE RUGBY WORLD CUP 2011

Played:	28
Won:	13
Lost:	14
Drawn:	1
Winning percentage:	46.4%
Points for:	619
Points against:	658
Points scored per match:	22.1
Points conceded per match:	23.5
Biggest victory:	58-7 v Brazil at Montevideo on May 1, 2013
Heaviest defeat:	65-9 v Argentina at Paysandu on May 17, 2014
World Rugby Ranking (at Jan 2015)	20

RUGBY WORLD CUP PERFORMANCES

1987	Did not enter
1991	Did not enter
1995	Did not qualify
1999	Pool stages
2003	Pool stages
2007	Did not qualify
2011	Did not qualify

Uruguay claimed the 20th and final place at Rugby World Cup 2015 when they overcame a narrow first-leg deficit to beat Russia 57-49 on aggregate in the final qualifying round. That success, which saw Uruguay roared on by a national record of more than 14,000 spectators at Montevideo's Estadio Charrúa in the second leg, means Los Teros will be gracing the finals for only the third time in their history. It also helped ease the pain of their agonising near-misses in qualification for Rugby World Cup 2007 and 2011, when they lost in the repechage finals to Portugal and Romania respectively.

Both of those European countries would end up being beaten in all four of their matches in the main event and Uruguay will be hoping to do better this time, although success in England is likely to be measured by the team's performances rather than results.

That is because Los Teros, whose side is largely made up of amateur players, have been drawn in one of the toughest-looking pools of any Rugby World Cup, one that includes former champions England and Australia as well as 2011 semi-finalists Wales. The other country in the pool, Fiji, appear to offer Uruguay their best chance of an upset but the Pacific Islanders have a reasonable record in Rugby World Cups and will also be expected to emerge victorious when the two teams face each other at Stadium MK in Milton Keynes on October 6.

If Uruguay do manage to upset the odds in one of those matches they would continue their proud record of winning at least once in each of their Rugby World Cup appearances, having beaten Spain in 1999 and Georgia in 2003. They have also been on the end of some huge defeats though, and it is that scenario they will be desperate to avoid this year. At Rugby World Cup 2003, they shipped 243 points in losing to South Africa (72-6), Samoa (60-13) and a heavy 111-13 loss to England, where the eventual champions ran in 17 tries in a devastating performance in Brisbane. That was comfortably the biggest defeat in Uruguay's 50-year Rugby history at the time — surpassed two years later by a 134-3 loss to South Africa — and capped a largely chastening Tournament for Diego Ormaechea's men.

Uruguay fared a little better in their Rugby World Cup debut four years earlier under Daniel Herrera, at least results-wise. In their first-ever match

COACH

PABLO LEMOINE

One of South American Rugby's most successful exports, Pablo Lemoine was a world-class performer as a player before moving into coaching. At more than 6ft and weighing almost 20st, Lemoine (pictured in his playing days at Rugby World Cup 1999) posed a formidable presence in the pack and, after attracting attention from Europe, the tough-tackling tighthead prop became Uruguay's first professional player when he joined Bristol in 1997. After a season in England, where he helped Bristol into the Premiership, Lemoine moved to Stade Français where he won the French title twice during a six-year spell. He called time on his international playing career in 2010 after winning 49 caps for Uruguay — including appearing at the Rugby World Cup in both 1999 and 2003 — before becoming national team coach in 2012.

STAR PLAYER

RODRIGO CAPO ORTEGA

Position:..Lock/flanker
Born:...December 8, 1980, Montevideo, Uruguay
Club:...Castres (Fra)
Height: 1.93m.......................................(6ft 5in)
Weight:.......................................101kg (224lb)
Caps:...38
Points:..45 (9t)

A veteran of Rugby World Cup 2003 and considered one of the best players in Uruguay's history, Rodrigo Capo Ortega returned to national team duty in 2014 after a five-year exile and helped his country book their RWC 2015 berth at the expense of Russia. The powerful and hugely experienced lock has been playing his club Rugby in France since 2002 – two years after making his Uruguay debut – and in 2013 helped Castres win the French title for only the fourth time. He was formerly Uruguay's captain and was also named as the new Castres skipper during the 2014/15 campaign.

among the world elite they picked up a victory, beating fellow newcomers Spain 27-15 after scoring two tries in the last three minutes, before being brought back down to earth by expected defeats to Scotland (43-12) and South Africa (39-3).

Bearing in mind they were up against professional opponents, Uruguay were far from disgraced in those two final matches, which came against the respective reigning Five Nations champions and reigning world champions. Now Los Teros will be hoping to ruffle a few feathers when they return to the big stage after an absence of more than a decade.

Uruguay's route to Rugby World Cup 2015 was three years in the making and involved matches against countries from all over the globe.

They beat Chile and Brazil to top the South American section and, after subsequently losing to the United States to once again find themselves involved in the repechage, Pablo Lemoine's troops saw off Hong Kong in the preliminary round.

That set up the showdown with Russia and, after losing the first leg 22-21 in Krasnoyarsk, Uruguay must have feared a third successive qualifying heartache. However, again aided by the boot of Felipe Berchesi, who converted 15 of his 18 attempts in the two legs for a personal haul of 42 points, plus three second-half tries, they turned things around in the second leg with a 36-27 victory to earn their place at Rugby World Cup 2015.

Coach Lemoine said: "From the day we board the plane to England to the moment our campaign ends, the whole Tournament is going to be an incredible experience for us.

"Playing big matches against big sides is an aspiration for all of our players, and thanks to the hard work we've put in we can all now look forward to competing on the Game's biggest stage. For Uruguayan Rugby this is the best gift imaginable."

PLAYERS TO WATCH

1. MATHIAS AROCENA
Age: 30; *Position:* fly-half; *Club:* Old Christians (Uru); *Caps:* 34; *Points:* 201 (8t, 25c, 36p, 1dg)

2. FELIPE BERCHESI
Age: 24; *Position:* fly-half; *Club:* Chambery (Fra); *Caps:* 12; *Points:* 83 (1t, 6c, 21p, 1dg)

3. NICOLÁS KLAPPENBACH
Age: 33; *Position:* hooker; *Club:* Champagnat (Uru); *Caps:* 38; *Points:* 10 (2t)

4. ALEJO CORRAL
Age: 33; *Position:* prop; *Club:* San Isidro (Arg); *Caps:* 33; *Points:* 15 (3t)

5. AGUSTÍN ORMAECHEA
Age: 24; *Position:* scrum-half; *Club:* Stade Montois (Fra); *Caps:* 16; *Points:* 89 (4t, 9c, 17p)

Uruguay in action against Hong Kong during their qualifying progamme

WESTERN SAMOA MAKE RWC HISTORY
OCTOBER 6, 1991, CARDIFF ARMS PARK

Wales had finished third in the inaugural Rugby World Cup in 1987 but four years on they were humbled by an unfancied Western Samoa side on home soil. Yet the Samoans had plenty of talent with Apollo Perelini, Brian Lima, Pat Lam and future All Blacks centre Frank Bunce in their ranks and their bone-shuddering tackling unsettled a Welsh side as To'o Vaega and Sila Vaifale crossed for tries in a 16-13 victory. The result at Cardiff Arms Park meant Wales failed to make it out of their pool while the Pacific Islanders, with a tiny player-base of around 2,000, made it through to the quarter-finals, where they lost to Scotland. It also led to one of Rugby's famous quips: "Thank heavens Wales weren't playing the whole of Samoa." Amazingly, Samoa repeated the feat at Rugby World Cup 1999 with a 38-31 victory in Cardiff.

To'o Vaega heads for the try line – he later named his son Cardiff in honour of the win

South Africa

The scope to play their most expansive attacking game in many years puts the Springboks firmly among the main contenders for glory at Rugby World Cup 2015. A new generation of playmakers will aim to add an extra dimension to a traditionally teak-hewn group of fierce natural competitors.

South Africa
www.sarugby.co.za

PLAYING STRIP Green shirts with gold trim, white shorts, green and gold socks

FORM SINCE RUGBY WORLD CUP 2011

Played:	37
Won:	26
Lost:	9
Drawn:	2
Winning percentage:	72.97%
Points for:	981
Points against:	633
Points scored per match:	26.51
Points conceded per match:	17.11
Biggest victory:	73-13 v Argentina at FNB Stadium, Soweto, on Aug 17, 2013
Heaviest defeat:	32-16 v New Zealand at FNB Stadium, Soweto, on Oct 6, 2012
World Rugby Ranking (at Jan 2015)	2

RUGBY WORLD CUP PERFORMANCES

1987	Did not enter
1991	Did not enter
1995	WORLD CHAMPIONS
1999	Semi-finals
2003	Quarter-finals
2007	WORLD CHAMPIONS
2011	Quarter-finals

South Africa breed them big and build them brutal, then challenge their playmakers to suck the life out of the intimidated and cowed. The Springboks have based their modern-era success around monster packs, all tight-five totems and back-row battlers. Throw in a scrum-half with a pinpoint pass and deadly box-kick, sprinkle over a fly-half who can sit in the pocket and fire a siege-gun boot, and the Boks generally have their recipe.

No amount of speed merchants or guileful centres can draw the eye away from the 10-man chokehold that underpinned their Rugby World Cup 1995 and 2007 triumphs. In 2011 the formula was found wanting though, as Australia edged out the Boks 11-9 in a Wellington quarter-final. Morné Steyn missed two shots at goal that night in New Zealand and, ever since, the Springboks have mused on the merits of expanding their traditional arm-wrestle methods.

Any backline boasting the savvy Jean de Villiers in the heart of midfield and the blistering Bryan Habana out wide cries out to be set free, so the thought momentum gathered, but it was not until South Africa gained their first win over New Zealand under coach Heyneke Meyer that the new breed of game-breaking fly-half finally arrived on the Springboks' top stage.

Handré Pollard's virtuoso two-try performance in the Boks' 27-25 victory over the All Blacks in Johannesburg in October 2014 ended New Zealand's 22-match unbeaten run. Not only that though, it also handed a nation a huge extra helping of Rugby World Cup hope. World Cup-winning Springbok luminaries like John Smit had warned the current crop of Test stars that only a pre-Tournament victory over the All Blacks could give Meyer's men the impetus required to claim glory in England in 2015. No sooner had the former Boks hooker asked than the current incumbents answered, with that stunning last-gasp victory courtesy of Pat Lambie's late penalty.

Pollard's gainline play that Rugby Championship day points the way to anyone wishing to expose the All Blacks. New Zealand have precious few weaknesses, but only England in autumn 2012 and South Africa in October 2014 had been able to get in behind their line and pull off victories up to that point since the All Blacks won Rugby World Cup 2011 on home soil. South Africa's game expansion then,

COACH

HEYNEKE MEYER

Heyneke Meyer rose through the high school and lower-level club coaching ranks before impressing with the SWD Eagles and then Northern Bulls. In 2002 he assumed overall control at the Blue Bulls, securing four Currie Cup titles in five years, and in 2007 he led the franchise to the first Super 14 title for any South African side. After a stint with Leicester Tigers, Meyer returned to South Africa and eventually succeeded Peter de Villiers as Springboks boss in 2012. Credited with steadying the Springbok ship after a turbulent period, he will demand South Africa do their position as a world superpower justice.

STAR PLAYER

BRYAN HABANA

Position:..Wing
Born:. June 12, 1983, Johannesburg, South Africa
Club:...Toulon (Fra)
Height:..............................1.80m (5ft 11in)
Weight:.............................94kg (207lb)
Caps:...106
Points:.....................................285 (57t)

South Africa's leading try-scorer remains one of the world's most potent finishers. This is the man who once raced a cheetah as a publicity stunt, but the notion of any contest in a foot race underscores Bryan Habana's status as one of the game's quickest. His eight tries in South Africa's triumphant Rugby World Cup 2007 campaign equalled the existing Tournament record. In statistics alone, Habana's record bears comparison with any of the all-time greats, and to sustain such speed, footwork and finishing power over a decade and more of Test Rugby is a feat in the increasingly mean modern era.

with chief cudgel Jonah Lomu literally taking Rugby to new heights. The powerhouse wing single-handedly brushed England aside, leaving just the All Blacks to deny South Africa the storybook finish.

The Springboks pulled off another stranglehold victory, edging out the Kiwis 15-12 in extra-time thanks to Joel Stransky's second drop goal in a try-less Final. Few begrudged the moment Mandela handed Francois Pienaar the Webb Ellis Cup, an exchange bathed in the hope of a nation's new dawn.

The Springboks have reached the knockout stages in every Tournament since, losing to Australia at the penultimate hurdle at Rugby World Cup 1999 before being dispatched in the last eight by New Zealand in 2003. Smit and company slugged their way past England 15-6 to gain glory once again in France at Rugby World Cup 2007, but were made to work far harder than anticipated after having comfortably overcome Brian Ashton's side 36-0 in pool action. Perhaps that 11-9 quarter-final defeat to Australia in 2011 can be viewed as South Africa's Rugby World Cup low point and, if so, it only indicates their lofty global standards and standing.

Should the Springboks turn that frustration into the motivation and catalyst for a 2015 resurgence, the rest of the world will do well to lace the armour of forewarning.

ought not be reliant on the man in the 10 shirt, more the measure of his mettle with ball in hand. Sit flat and offer options, and suddenly the Springboks are an entirely new, and ever more dangerous, proposition.

For the northern hemisphere and hosts England especially, this could be tricky to stomach given the widespread acceptance that, since 2011, the Springboks have been the side to stay closest to the near-peerless New Zealanders.

Sporting exile denied South Africa entry to Rugby World Cup 1987 and 1991 but their debut was pure fairytale stuff. The Rainbow Nation hosted the world in 1995, with the significance of Nelson Mandela sporting the Springbok shirt with pride chief among the Tournament's many poetic snapshots. New Zealand ravaged all before them

PLAYERS TO WATCH

1. EBEN ETZEBETH
Age: 23; *Position:* lock; *Club:* Stormers (RSA); *Caps:* 33; *Points:* 0
2. HANDRÉ POLLARD
Age: 21; *Position:* fly-half; Club: Bulls (RSA); *Caps:* 9; *Points:* 65 (2t, 14c, 8p, 1dg)
3. TENDAI MTAWARIRA
Age: 29; *Position:* prop; *Club:* Sharks (RSA); *Caps:* 64; *Points:* 10 (2t)
4. JEAN DE VILLIERS
Age: 34; *Position:* centre; *Club:* Stormers (RSA); *Caps:* 106; *Points:* 135 (27t)
5. FRANCOIS HOUGAARD
Age: 27; *Position:* scrum-half; *Club:* Bulls (RSA); *Caps:* 35; *Points:* 25 (5t)

South Africa head to England seeking a third Rugby World Cup triumph

Samoa

Western Samoa were quarter-finalists at the Rugby World Cup in 1991 and 1995, a remarkable achievement for the Pacific Islanders. Although Samoa have yet to return to those heady heights, their style of play makes them worldwide crowd-pleasers, as does their regular success in causing upsets against big-name rivals.

It started so well for Samoa on the Rugby World Cup stage. After not being invited to participate in the inaugural 1987 Tournament, they shocked the Rugby world by beating Wales on their own turf on their way to the quarter-finals at Rugby World Cup 1991.

Described as 'minnows' beforehand, somewhat mistakenly given they had future All Blacks Frank Bunce and Stephen Bachop in their side, Western Samoa left Cardiff Arms Park 16-13 victors thanks to tries from Sila Vaifale and To'o Vaega, who also added a conversion and two penalties. The victory was celebrated unequivocally back in Apia and its importance is illustrated by the fact Vaega commemorated the result by later naming his newborn son Cardiff.

Buoyed by causing one of the greatest upsets in their first ever Rugby World Cup match, Western Samoa were too strong for Argentina, 35-12, then lost a hard-fought encounter to eventual champions Australia 9-3 to finish second in their pool. Scotland proved to be one challenge too many, ending their remarkable run with a 28-6 triumph in their Murrayfield quarter-final, but by then Western Samoa had endeared themselves to the Rugby fraternity thanks to their ferocious forward play and expansive running game.

Western Samoa entered Rugby World Cup 1995 in confident mood after beating Wales once again in 1994 and wins over Italy and Argentina helped them finish runners-up in Pool B behind England. A quarter-final clash against South Africa ensued but Western Samoa were put to the sword, losing 42-14 to a Springbok side that would overcome the odds to win the Rugby World Cup at their first attempt. Any hopes of making

it three quarter-final appearances in a row in 1999 were dashed when, under the guidance of All Black great and former Western Samoa assistant coach Bryan Williams, the now-rechristened Samoa slumped to a pool defeat to Argentina but then ran in five tries to beat Wales and finish runners-up in Pool D. Second place saw Samoa qualify for the quarter-final play-off round and Scotland, for the second time in Rugby World Cup history, ended their interest as Kenny Logan inspired them to a 35-20 win at Murrayfield.

Samoa can count themselves unfortunate not to have progressed beyond the pool stages at the next

COACH

STEPHEN BETHAM

Stephen Betham is one of the most hard-working coaches in world Rugby and has turned his hand to Test Rugby after considerable success in Sevens, having led Samoa to the Sevens World Series title in 2010. In 2012 he succeeded Titimaea Tafua as coach of Samoa's 15-a-side team and has presided over impressive victories against teams such as Wales, Scotland and Italy in his three years at the helm. A renowned skills coach and keen student of the game, Betham likes his side to play free-flowing, attacking Rugby and expects his players to entertain as well as put points on the board.

Samoa
www.samoarugbyunion.ws

PLAYING STRIP Blue shirts, white shorts, blue socks

FORM SINCE RUGBY WORLD CUP 2011

Played:	19
Won:	10
Lost:	8
Drawn:	1
Winning percentage:	55.26
Points for:	397
Points against:	408
Points scored per match:	20.89
Points conceded per match:	21.47
Biggest victory:	39-10 v Italy in Mbombela on June 15, 2013
Heaviest defeat:	56-23 v South Africa in Pretoria on June 22, 2013
World Rugby Ranking (at Jan 2015)	10

RUGBY WORLD CUP PERFORMANCES

1987	Did not enter
1991	Quarter-finals
1995	Quarter-finals
1999	Quarter-final play-offs
2003	Pool stages
2007	Pool stages
2011	Pool stages

STAR PLAYER

GEORGE PISI

Position:..Centre/full-back
Born:..............................June 29, 1986, Apia, Samoa
Club:...Northampton (Eng)
Height:..185cm (6ft 1in)
Weight:..94kg (207lb)
Caps:...17
Points:..15 (3t)

A fast, skilful and powerful centre equally adept with ball in hand or in defence, Pisi won plenty of admirers in four seasons with Auckland-based Super Rugby franchise the Blues before swapping hemispheres and joining Top 14 side Clermont for a short stint in 2011. He joined Northampton later that year and his time in the Premiership has been a big success. Pisi scooped the Saints Players' Player and Supporters' Player of the Season awards in his debut season and in 2014 helped his side win the Premiership title with a try in the final against Saracens.

PLAYERS TO WATCH

1. DAVID LEMI
Age: 33; *Position:* wing; *Club:* Bristol (Eng); *Caps:* 42; *Points:* 55 (11t)
2. ALAPATI LEIUA
Age: 26; *Position:* centre/wing; *Club:* Wasps (Eng); *Caps:* 10; *Points:* 10 (2t)
3. TJ IOANE
Age: 26; *Position:* flanker/No. 8; *Club:* Highlanders (NZL); *Caps:* 2; *Points:* 0
4. JOE TEKORI
Age: 31; *Position:* flanker; *Club:* Toulouse (Fra) *Caps:* 28; *Points:* 20 (4t)
5. KANE THOMPSON
Age: 33; *Position:* lock; *Club:* Newcastle (Eng); *Caps:* 31; *Points:* 10 (2t)

Samoa kick off their Rugby World Cup 2015 campaign against the United States in Brighton on September 20, before heading north to Birmingham to tackle South Africa – amazingly for the fourth Rugby World Cup in succession – six days later. Rugby World Cup 2019 hosts Japan are their opponents on October 3 in Milton Keynes and, all being well, they then face Scotland a week later in Newcastle in a match likely to determine who finishes Pool B runner-up and clinches a quarter-final spot. A third quarter-final appearance is a distinct possibility given Samoa ended 2014 only two places behind Scotland in 10th in the World Rugby Rankings and boast seasoned Premiership, Super Rugby and Top 14 players in the form of George Pisi, Joe Tekori, James Johnston, Daniel Leo and Sakaria Taulafo.

With one eye on Rugby World Cup 2015, coach Stephen Betham named a mixture of youth and experience in his squad for end-of-year Tests against Italy, Canada and England. TJ Ioane's inclusion was one call-up to get Samoa fans excited as the powerhouse loose forward was in terrorising form during the 2014 Super Rugby season as the Highlanders shocked many by reaching the knockout stages. Ioane's lung-busting displays around the breakdown had seen him tipped by many to force his way into the All Blacks reckoning but, given he is 25 years old, he has opted for the country of birth, and Steve Hansen's loss is Betham's gain.

three Rugby World Cups given the draws were not kind. There could be no complaints in 2003 and 2007 when they were in pools featuring England and South Africa, who would go on to win the respective Tournaments. It did not get any easier in 2011 when they faced the Springboks in pool action for a third successive Rugby World Cup and also came up against an in-form Wales side that were eager to exact revenge for the 1991 and 1999 defeats.

Morale-boosting wins over Namibia and Fiji helped to restore some pride but the disappointment was evident as, for the third Rugby World Cup running, the Samoans made an early exit.

Samoa won the Pacific Nations Cup in 2012 and topped their conference in 2014, book-ending wins over Wales (2012), Scotland (2013) and Italy (2013, 2014). And they have the small matter of a first home Test against the mighty All Blacks on July 8 to contend with.

Samoa have not progressed beyond the pool stages since Rugby World Cup 1999

Scotland

Scotland are certainly not short of ambition after they stated their target for Rugby World Cup 2015 is to lift the Webb Ellis Cup. That would mark a huge improvement after their disappointment four years ago and, following a period of transition, New Zealander Vern Cotter's leadership skills will be firmly put to the test.

Scotland are a familiar presence in the knockout stages of the Rugby World Cup and will now look to raise their game once more to defy recent form and improve on their 2011 showing.

The Scots have rarely had any trouble progressing from their pool and it was only four years ago in New Zealand that they first failed to escape the pool section. As well as being quarter-finalists on five occasions, they even came within a try of reaching the Rugby World Cup 1991 Final, only to snatch defeat from the jaws of victory as England claimed the semi-final win.

But these are changed days and Scotland must produce some improved performances if they are to reach the latter stages of the competition. Their Six Nations form does not bode well and they have not lifted the championship since Italy joined 16 years ago, while their last five-team title in 1999 has been followed by 54 defeats from the 74 matches played up to the end of the 2014 event.

Coach Vern Cotter will pin his hopes on the fact that Scotland have always lifted themselves for the challenge of competing on a global stage. Had they not run into the might of the All Blacks in three of their first four quarter-final appearances, Scotland's Rugby World Cup history might have made for more impressive reading. In 1987, at the inaugural Rugby World Cup, they managed an entertaining 20-20 draw with France, followed by resounding wins over Zimbabwe (60-21) and Romania (55-28), before the quality of the co-hosts New Zealand saw them sink to a 30-3 defeat in the last eight.

Four years later and buoyed by their 1990 Five Nations Grand Slam, Scotland marched into Rugby World Cup 1991 with an obvious streak of confidence in their stride. Japan (47-9), Zimbabwe (51-12) and Ireland (24-15) were all swatted aside by Ian McGeechan's team as they topped Pool B and set up another quarter-final tie, this time with Western Samoa. The Pacific Islanders proved no match either and a 28-6 victory put skipper David Sole and Co on course for a battle with the Auld Enemy. But even home advantage could not give them the spark they required and, after Gavin Hastings missed a simple kick with the game tied at 6-6, England scraped an ugly 9-6 win at Murrayfield to deny Scotland their golden chance.

If that was the high point, the decline in Scottish Rugby did not appear immediately obvious. A then record 89-0 victory over the Ivory Coast

COACH

VERN COTTER

Scotland supporters will hope former Clermont Auvergne boss Vern Cotter can repeat the magic formula that saw him transform the unfashionable French outfit into one of the strongest sides in Europe. When Cotter took over at the Parc des Sports Marcel Michelin in 2006, he found a club mired in mid-table mediocrity. Within two years, he had taken them to the Top 14 final and masterminded a European Challenge Cup win before helping them become champions of France a year later. Only a Jonny Wilkinson-inspired Toulon prevented him from capping his club coaching career with a Heineken Cup triumph in 2013 as Clermont lost the all-French final 16-15 at Twickenham. Now as coach of Scotland, the New Zealander has just as big a job turning around the nation's fortunes.

Scotland
www.scottishrugby.org

PLAYING STRIP Blue shirts with white collar, white shorts, blue socks

FORM SINCE RUGBY WORLD CUP 2011

Played:	34
Won:	13
Lost:	21
Drawn:	0
Winning percentage:	38.2%
Points for:	596
Points against:	809
Points scored per match:	16.74
Points conceded per match:	23.79
Biggest victory:	42-17 v Japan at Murrayfield on November 9, 2013
Heaviest defeat:	55-6 v South Africa in Port Elizabeth on June 28, 2014
World Rugby Ranking (at Jan 2015)	8

RUGBY WORLD CUP PERFORMANCES

1987	Quarter-finals
1991	Semi-finals
1995	Quarter-finals
1999	Quarter-finals
2003	Quarter-finals
2007	Quarter-finals
2011	Pool stages

STAR PLAYER

STUART HOGG

Position:..Full-back
Born:...................June 24, 1992, Melrose, Scotland
Club:...................................Glasgow Warriors (Sco)
Height:...1.83m (6ft 0in)
Weight:..83.5kg (184lb)
Caps:..27
Points:...43 (8t, 1p)

Brought up in the Rugby heartlands of the Borders, Stuart Hogg is the genuine world-class talent in the Scotland squad. A product of the famous Hawick club and a distant relative of Manchester United icon George Best, he made his Glasgow debut aged 18. He won his first Scotland cap two years later and quickly established himself as Scotland's first pick at 15. His displays during the 2013 Six Nations — including tries against England and Italy — earned him a place as the youngest member of the British and Irish Lions squad which travelled to Australia.

Scotland failed to reach the knockout stages for the first time in 2011

once again through to the knockout rounds. This time, though, it was hosts Australia providing the roadblock on Scottish ambitions as the team were left down and out Down Under by a 33-16 defeat.

Yet Frank Hadden's side should have restored some gloss to Scotland's Rugby World Cup record four years later in France. The coach controversially fielded a second-string XV against New Zealand as he rested key men but the move paid off as wins over Portugal (56-10), Romania (42-0) and Italy (18-16) saw them into the last eight, but against surprise package Argentina, they missed out on another semi-final as they went down 19-13 in Paris.

If that was heartbreaking, it barely compares to the pain endured in New Zealand at Rugby World Cup 2011. Scotland squeezed past Romania 34-24 and Georgia 15-6 before suffering a narrow 13-12 loss, once again to Argentina. With qualification hopes hanging by a thread, Scotland faced England in a decider needing an eight-point win to progress. England were below par but still had enough to claim a 16-12 win as Scotland's proud record of at least making the knockout stages in every Rugby World Cup ended.

With South Africa, Samoa, Japan and the United States lying in wait, they will have to recapture some of that old swagger to clamber out of the pool.

opened Rugby World Cup 1995 before a 41-5 victory over Tonga meant the Scots could afford to lose to France 22-19 in their final pool fixture. They even managed to push the All Blacks close before going down 48-30 in the quarter-finals as they went out.

The quarter-finals were again reached at Rugby World Cup 1999 as crushing wins over Uruguay (43-12) and Spain (48-0) teed up a play-off with Samoa after the Scots bounced back from

a 46-29 defeat in their opener with the Springboks. With the Samoans beaten 35-20, Scotland once again found themselves lining up against New Zealand in the last eight but the result was the same as always as they slumped 30-18 in Edinburgh.

France claimed another pool-stage win at Rugby World Cup 2003 as they recorded a 51-9 victory, but with Japan (32-11), United States (39-15) and Fij (22-20) dispensed with, Scotland were

PLAYERS TO WATCH

1. GREIG LAIDLAW
Age: 29; *Position:* scrum-half; *Club:* Gloucester (Eng); *Caps:* 34; *Points:* 299 (3t, 37c, 70p)

2. MATT SCOTT
Age: 24; *Position:* centre; *Club:* Edinburgh (Sco); *Caps:* 21; *Points:* 15 (3t)

3. RICHIE GRAY
Age: 25; *Position:* lock; *Club:* Castres (Fra); *Caps:* 42; *Points:* 10 (2t)

4. JOHNNIE BEATTIE
Age: 29; *Position:* number 8; *Club:* Castres (Fra); *Caps:* 34; *Points:* 15 (3t)

5. TIM VISSER
Age: 28; *Position:* wing; *Club:* Edinburgh (Sco); *Caps:* 15; *Points:* 35 (7t)

Japan

Participants in every Rugby World Cup, Japan enter RWC 2015 following an outstanding year. The Brave Blossoms may have recorded only one win in 24 games on Rugby's greatest stage and, while they have yet to reach the knockout stages, the RWC 2019 hosts remain one of the most entertaining sides in the world Game.

Japan
www.jrfu.org

PLAYING STRIP Red and white shirts, black shorts, black socks

FORM SINCE RUGBY WORLD CUP 2011

Played:	33
Won:	24
Lost:	9
Drawn:	0
Winning percentage:	72.72
Points for:	1,489
Points against:	540
Points scored per match:	45.1
Points conceded per match:	16.4
Biggest victory:	132-10 v Sri Lanka in Nagoya on May 10, 2014
Heaviest defeat:	54-6 v New Zealand in Tokyo on November 2, 2013
World Rugby Ranking (at Jan 2015)	11

RUGBY WORLD CUP PERFORMANCES

1987	Pool stages
1991	Pool stages
1995	Pool stages
1999	Pool stages
2003	Pool stages
2007	Pool stages
2011	Pool stages

Despite boasting more Rugby clubs than any other nation in the world, Japan conceded 21 tries in three matches to finish rock-bottom of their group at Rugby World Cup 1987. Comprehensive defeats to Scotland and Ireland in their first two pool matches suggested Japan were in for another wooden-spoon finish at Rugby World Cup 1991 but, in their final round-robin match, the Brave Blossoms got off the mark in fine style, running in nine tries in a 52-8 victory against Zimbabwe to finish third in Pool Two.

Any hopes of building on that at Rugby World Cup 1995 were dashed in South Africa when Japan were pitted against three powerful nations, New Zealand, Ireland and Wales, in the toughest pool. Japan shipped 14 tries in defeats to Wales and Ireland before conceding 21 in the 145-17 loss to a second-string New Zealand side in Bloemfontein to finish bottom once again. It got worse four years later at Rugby World Cup 1999 when they managed a meagre two tries in three matches to prop up their pool once again, and in 2003 when their four pool losses yielded only six touchdowns.

All Black great John Kirwan was appointed as Japan's head coach in 2006 and guided them to their first positive Rugby World Cup result in 16 years when a last-minute conversion from Shotaro Onishi earned them a 12-12 draw with Canada. The end of a 13-game losing run at this level was obviously a welcome relief to all those involved with Japanese Rugby, but their narrow 35-31 defeat by Fiji was arguably more impressive. It suggested that, at long last, Japan were no longer the sport's perennial whipping boys.

Japan went into Rugby World Cup 2011 in confident mood having scooped their first ever Pacific Nations Cup title a few months earlier and risen to 13th in the World Rugby Rankings. Their disappointment at drawing with Canada and narrowly losing to Tonga illustrated the progress they had made under Kirwan in his five years in charge, while further losses to New Zealand and France were to be expected.

Critics would point to four consecutive victories over Tonga and a pair of wins against Canada since the last Rugby World Cup as justifiable cause for being disheartened with Japan's 2011 showing but, given that Tonga beat eventual runners-up France in pool action, the negativity towards Kirwan's charges was perhaps unfair. The Japan RFU turned to Eddie Jones when Kirwan chose not

COACH

EDDIE JONES

Eddie Jones gave up teaching in 1994 to become a full-time Rugby coach and given that he has enjoyed more than 20 years of success in both club and international Rugby, it was an astute decision. Jones guided the ACT Brumbies to the Super 12 title in 2001 and was subsequently appointed Australia coach. He led the Wallabies to the Rugby World Cup 2003 Final, where they lost in extra-time to Clive Woodward's England. Jones assisted South Africa to RWC glory in 2007 and after stints at Saracens and Suntory Sungoliath, he became Japan coach in 2012. Ten straight wins from November 2013 to November 2014 suggest Jones is set to lead the Brave Blossoms into a promising new era.

STAR PLAYER

AYUMU GOROMARU

Position:	Full-back
Born:	March 1, 1986, Fukuoka, Japan
Club:	Yamaha Jubilo (Jpn)
Height:	185cm (6ft 1in)
Weight:	98kg (216lb)
Caps:	43
Points:	532 (15t, 131c, 65p)

Mitsutake Hagimoto gave Ayumu Goromaru his international debut in 2005 at the age of 19 after impressive displays for Yamaha Jubilo. After being dropped by Hagimoto's successor Jean-Pierre Elissalde, the specialist kicker was recalled when John Kirwan took over in 2009 but once again found himself in the wilderness when he did not make Japan's squad for Rugby World Cup 2011. Goromaru has since made Japan's full-back jersey his own and averages 12.3 points per match – a higher average points-per-game haul than the likes of Morné Steyn, Ronan O'Gara and Percy Montgomery.

Rankings during that run. Expectation is subsequently high and Japanese fans will be impressed by Jones' assertion that quarter-final qualification is within their grasp this time.

"Our target is to make the quarter-finals of the next Rugby World Cup, and people think we're crazy for saying that," Jones told the *Japan Times*. "But people thought we were crazy three years ago saying we would make the top 10, and we have. That's a fantastic achievement for Japan."

Japan may no longer be able to call on international Rugby's all-time leading try-scorer, Daisuke Ohata, who retired prior to Rugby World Cup 2011, but they still have a whole host of players with the necessary guile and pace to breach even the most resolute of defences. Scrum-half Fumiaki Tanaka is as tricky as they come and even kept first-choice All Blacks half-back Aaron Smith out of the Highlanders side for a brief spell during the 2013 Super Rugby season. Tanaka and fly-half Harumichi Tatekawa are the perfect foil for the back three of Kenki Fukuoka, Akihito Yamada and Ayumu Goromaru.

Japan will host Rugby World Cup 2019 and, regardless of results this year, Rugby is destined to become even more popular there in the coming years.

to renew his contract at the end of 2011 and the former Australia coach has picked up where his predecessor left off. Jones, who guided the Wallabies to the 2003 Final where they lost in extra-time to England, proved to be an inspired choice when appointed in April 2012.

His success included 10 straight wins from 2013 to 2014, including one against Italy. Jones suffered a stroke towards the end of 2013 but recovered to lead Japan to the top of their Pacific Nations Cup conference the following year and a high of ninth in the World Rugby

PLAYERS TO WATCH

1. FUMIAKI TANAKA
Age: 30; *Position:* scrum-half; *Club:* Highlanders (NZL); *Caps:* 44; *Points:* 40 (8t).

2. HENDRIK TUI
Age: 27; *Position:* flanker; *Club:* Queensland Reds (Aus); *Caps:* 27; *Points:* 55 (11t)

3. TAKASHI KIKUTANI
Age: 35; *Position:* flanker/No. 8; *Club:* Canon Eagles (Jpn); *Caps:* 68; *Points:* 160 (32t)

4. MICHAEL LEITCH
Age: 26; *Position:* flanker/No. 8; *Club:* Toshiba Brave Lupus (Jpn); *Caps:* 38; *Points:* 55 (11t)

5. HARUMICHI TATEKAWA
Age: 25; *Position:* fly-half/centre; *Club:* Brumbies (Aus); *Caps:* 28; *Points:* 46 (6t, 8c)

Japanese players celebrate a famous win over Wales in 2013

United States

The United States have been regular participants at the Rugby World Cup, appearing in every Tournament, except for the 1995 edition. The sport is on the rise back home though, spurred on by its Olympic return, and the Eagles are hoping to cash in on the growing momentum.

It is a little-known fact that the United States are the defending Olympic champions in Rugby. Of course Rugby has not featured at an Olympic Games since 1924 but, with the Sevens version of the Game on the agenda for Rio 2016, the Eagles have found a new surge of interest and enthusiasm for both forms of the sport at home and

USA RUGBY

United States
www.usarugby.org

PLAYING STRIP Dark blue and red shirts, dark blue shorts, dark blue socks.

FORM SINCE RUGBY WORLD CUP 2011
Played:	24
Won:	8
Lost:	15
Drawn:	1
Winning percentage:	35.4%
Points for:	482
Points against:	608
Points scored per match:	20.1
Points conceded per match:	25.3
Biggest victory:	34-3 v Romania in Bucharest on November 24, 2012
Heaviest defeat:	74-6 v New Zealand in Chicago on November 1, 2014
World Rugby Ranking (at Jan 2015)	16

RUGBY WORLD CUP PERFORMANCES
1987	Pool stages
1991	Pool stages
1995	Did not qualify
1999	Pool stages
2003	Pool stages
2007	Pool stages
2011	Pool stages

COACH

MIKE TOLKIN

After a series of international coaches, the United States turned to one of their own in 2012, just as their squad was growing ever more cosmopolitan in its experiences. Tolkin was promoted from the role of defensive coach after his unit performed well at Rugby World Cup 2011, but his experience with the Eagles runs much deeper. The New Yorker, coach of the New York Athletic Club until 2011, has been involved with the national programme since his early 20s, helping to set up the Under-19 team back in 1992 and later working to scout and develop young talent.

are looking to channel that into their Rugby World Cup 2015 campaign.

A nation that can count its total number of Rugby World Cup wins on one hand has never been short of optimism or confidence and although that may not be enough to ensure a prolonged campaign in England, an increasing number of the squad playing professionally in Europe means this is the most intriguing United States team in living memory. Competition for that title, admittedly, is in short supply. The sport continues to be a minority one in the USA where the likes of American football, baseball and basketball enjoy most of the media's attention, and development has understandably been slow as a result.

After being invited to participate in the first ever Rugby World Cup in 1987, the United States promptly won their first match, edging out Japan 21-18 on the back of 13 points from Ray Nelson, but heavy defeats to New Zealand and England followed along with an early flight home. The experience benefited the team all the same and they put together some solid results in the intervening years before earning qualification for the 1991 Tournament, but a tough draw alongside New Zealand, England and Italy offered little hope and three resounding defeats were the inevitable result.

They missed out entirely in 1995 – the only time they have failed to qualify – after a pair of narrow losses to Argentina in the qualifying Tournament, although

they almost enjoyed a major scalp in 1993 when they pushed Australia all the way before losing 26-22 at Riverside.

They were back at Rugby World Cup 1999, in Pool E with Ireland, Australia and Romania. After losing to the Irish, their only decent shot at a win was against Romania but a 27-25 defeat ensured another winless campaign. But their Tournament was not a total failure – in losing 55-19 to Australia they were the only team to score a try against the eventual champions.

Four Test wins in a row – the Eagles' best ever run – saw the United States

STAR PLAYER

CHRIS WYLES

Position:................Full-back/wing/centre
Born:.........................September 13, 1983
              Stamford, Connecticut, United States
Club:..............................Saracens (Eng)
Height:.........................1.83m (6ft 2in)
Weight:.........................93kg (205lb)
Caps:.......................................45
Points:...............212 (14t, 23c, 31p, 1dg)

Born in the United States to English parents, Wyles moved across the Atlantic at the age of 11 and emerged as a professional player for Nottingham after studying at the city's university. He moved on to Northampton in 2006 before his performances for the United States at Rugby World Cup 2007 caught the eye of Eddie Jones, who took him to Saracens the following year. The versatile back has shifted from wing to centre for his club after returning from injury, but has been a stalwart at full-back for his country.

go into Rugby World Cup 2003 with a surge of momentum and they rode it into a 13-3 lead over Fiji early in the second half, only to lose the opener 19-18. A loss to Scotland in their second pool match made it 10 Rugby World Cup defeats in a row, but they rebounded to beat Japan 39-26 on the back of 17 points from Mike Hercus before signing off with defeat to France. Four years later, the Eagles went into Rugby

World Cup 2007 ranked 13th in the world, but swiftly lost all four games against England, Samoa, South Africa and Tonga. As in 1999, though, there was one silver lining, with Takudzwa Ngwenya collecting Try of the Year honours after out-running Springboks speedster Bryan Habana to score in the 64-15 loss to South Africa.

While the 2007 squad had included a couple of English-based players and a handful from France, by the time Rugby World Cup 2011 rolled around the experience in the group was growing thanks to the likes of Chris Biller (Bath), Paul Emerick (Wasps), Hayden Smith and Chris Wyles (both Saracens).

However, poor results in the warm-ups – including losses to Japan – tempered expectations with the team drawn against Ireland, Russia, Australia and Italy, with victory over Russia the barometer for success. They duly secured it, 13-6, thanks to a try from Mike Petri, and while an impressive defensive display limited the damage to 22-10 against Ireland, they were blown out by Australia and comfortably beaten by Italy before heading home.

That European-based contingent has grown again going into this year's Tournament and, of the squad which played in their qualifying matches against Uruguay, 14 of the 26 were playing professionally overseas including 10 of them in England.

The United States have been putting their increased experience to good use, recording victories over Georgia, Romania and Russia in the build-up to Rugby World Cup 2015, creeping back up the rankings in the process.

With the draw putting them up against South Africa, Scotland, Samoa and Japan, there is hope that this can be the year they record multiple wins at a Rugby World Cup for the first time.

The United States are yet to reach the knockout stages at a Rugby World Cup

PLAYERS TO WATCH

1. ERIC FRY
Age: 27; *Position:* prop; *Club:* Newcastle (Eng); *Caps:* 27; *Points:* 15 (3t)
2. SCOTT LAVALLA
Age: 26; *Position:* flanker; *Club:* Stade Français (Fra); *Caps:* 29; *Points:* 5 (1t)
3. BLAINE SCULLY
Age: 27; *Position:* wing; *Club:* Leicester (Eng); *Caps:* 21; *Points:* 35 (7t)
4. CAM DOLAN
Age: 25; *Position:* number 8; *Club:* Northampton (Eng); *Caps:* 10; *Points:* 10 (2t)
5. HAYDEN SMITH
Age: 30; *Position:* lock; *Club:* Saracens (Eng); *Caps:* 22; *Points:* 0

A NATION UNIFIED
JUNE 24, 1995, ELLIS PARK, JOHANNESBURG

Still the Rugby World Cup by which all others are measured, the 1995 Tournament was more than a sporting event, it was a political milestone. The abolition of apartheid had seen South Africa readmitted to the international fraternity and they were rewarded by being named host nation for Rugby's showpiece event. Carried forward on a wave of emotion, the Springboks beat champions Australia in their opening match and never looked back. They were nevertheless the underdogs in the Final against New Zealand and Rugby's first global icon in Jonah Lomu, but they tamed the beast to win in extra-time. Nelson Mandela presented Francois Pienaar with the Webb Ellis Cup in arguably the most iconic moment in the history of the Game.

South Africa captain Francois Pienaar receives the Webb Ellis Cup from Nelson Mandela

New Zealand

The reigning champions have grown even stronger since lifting the Webb Ellis Cup for the second time in 2011 and will begin their title defence as clear favourites. The All Blacks have few weaknesses and are ruthlessly efficient, yet their history of imploding beneath the pressure of Rugby World Cups could make them vulnerable.

ALL BLACKS

New Zealand
www.allblacks.com

PLAYING STRIP Black shirts, black shorts, black socks

FORM SINCE RUGBY WORLD CUP 2011

Played:	42
Won:	38
Lost:	2
Drawn:	2
Winning percentage:	92.85%
Points for:	1,353
Points against:	665
Points scored per match:	32.21
Points conceded per match:	15.83
Biggest victory:	74-6 v United States at Chicago on November 1, 2014
Heaviest defeat:	38-21 v England at Twickenham on December 1, 2012
World Rugby Ranking (at Jan 2015)	1

RUGBY WORLD CUP PERFORMANCES

1987	WORLD CHAMPIONS
1991	Semi-finals
1995	Runners-up
1999	Semi-finals
2003	Semi-finals
2007	Quarter-finals
2011	WORLD CHAMPIONS

New Zealand should sweep all before them at Rugby World Cup 2015 based on form in recent years.

The champions have compiled a formidable record since 2011 which has seen their aura of invincibility rarely challenged. To hand them back the Webb Ellis Cup now, though, would be to overlook history and the psychology that can weigh heavily on All Black shoulders when it comes to honouring their perennial dominance of the Game by winning the greatest prize of all.

It is said the only team that can beat New Zealand are New Zealand themselves, and that is especially pertinent at Rugby World Cups.

The first of the All Blacks' two crowns came at the inaugural Tournament in 1987 with the co-hosts, who included all-time greats such as John Kirwan, Michael Jones and Grant Fox in their ranks, barely challenged en route to the Final, where they crushed France 29-9.

Four years later and Rugby World Cup was a different animal altogether, becoming a truly global event. The *laissez-faire* approach many teams had adopted in 1987 was gone. On this occasion New Zealand were denied by the all-round brilliance of Nick Farr-Jones' Australia, but could rightfully claim to be the second best team having dispatched runners-up England 18-12 in the pool stage.

It was Rugby World Cup 1995 that first gave birth to the 'chokers' stamp that continues to haunt the sport's dominant force. With Jonah Lomu leading the charge, they amassed 222 points in three pool matches before swatting aside Scotland and England to set up a Final against South Africa. Even the hosts looked ready to fall before Sean Fitzpatrick's All Blacks but they eventually prevailed 15-12 in extra-time.

'Choking' was the only explanation for their performance at Rugby World Cup 1999 when, having overwhelmed England at Twickenham in a key pool game, the favourites allowed a 24-10 semi-final lead against France to deteriorate into a 43-31 loss in one of the great games in Rugby World Cup history. New Zealand were clearly dazed as France ran in 33 points, unable to issue any response.

At least at Rugby World Cup 2003 the All Blacks were not favourites. That honour went to Martin Johnson's England, the eventual winners. Having blazed an unstoppable path to the semi-finals, beating South Africa along the way, New Zealand came unstuck

COACH

STEVE HANSEN

Steve Hansen was appointed Graham Henry's successor as New Zealand head coach after the Rugby World Cup 2011 triumph. Hansen's path has followed Henry's closely. In 2002 he replaced his compatriot as Wales coach before joining the All Blacks management team two years later, primarily as forwards coach. New Zealand's demise at Rugby World Cup 2007 placed the coaching team's position in grave doubt, but the decision to retain them was rewarded with the Webb Ellis Cup four years later. Hansen attracted his fair share of criticism, but once Henry stepped down he was the obvious choice to lead the All Blacks.

STAR PLAYER

KIERAN READ

Position:	Number 8
Born:	October 26, 1985
	Papakura, New Zealand
Club:	Canterbury (NZL)
Height:	1.93m (6ft 3in)
Weight:	111kg (244lb)
Caps:	72
Points:	85 (17t)

In a team populated by stars, it is Kieran Read who stands out as the most influential of all. The Crusaders number 8 is the complete player, combining remarkable handling skills and vision with a hard edge when battling in the trenches. He is lethal when roaming out wide, using his athleticism to create openings and soft hands to complete some remarkable offloads that create try-scoring opportunities. Read may be a back-rower, but he has the speed of thought of a three-quarter in attack.

team on the day so the New Zealand public had feelings of both delight and relief after an 8-7 victory ended the All Blacks' 24-year wait for a second Rugby World Cup success.

By any yardstick, the irrepressible All Blacks should retain the Webb Ellis Cup. In number 8 Kieran Read they have the sport's finest player, and in wing Julian Savea the most deadly of strike runners. Aaron Smith is irrepressible at scrum-half, while old warrior Richie McCaw is as indomitable as ever.

They frequently dazzle, producing breathtaking examples of skill, yet it is the fundamentals of the Game at which New Zealand truly excel. Expertly turning the screw, they build pressure before pouncing on errors with surgical efficiency in a tactical approach that is more calculating than swashbuckling. They kick more than most and leak tries, but their ability to respond by plundering tries in quick succession and conjure the moment of magic required to settle tight games are the hallmarks of their genius. For all their myriad of strengths, though, history points to a mental fragility at Rugby World Cups. Triumphing on home soil in 2011 may have addressed that frailty, and it now remains to be seen whether that success is the start of a period of All Blacks dominance.

Reigning champions New Zealand will again be the team to beat at Rugby World Cup 2015

against hosts Australia in a 22-10 defeat that underlined their fragility in the knockout stages.

The nation's worst fears were realised when the extraordinary events of 1999 were repeated at Rugby World Cup 2007. Once again the pool stage was a formality with 309 points scored in four games, only for France to intervene when it really mattered. Trailing 13-3 and in danger of unravelling, France fought back to win 20-18. Shell-

shock was evident once more as the All Blacks lost their senses, refusing to attempt the drop goal that would propel them into the semi-finals.

New Zealand's ability to hold their nerve was again tested when they hosted Rugby World Cup 2011. The best team in the Tournament by some margin, they were firm favourites to triumph in the Final when, once again, they came up against France. Their familiar foes were arguably the better

PLAYERS TO WATCH

1. RICHIE McCAW
Age: 34; *Position:* back row; *Club:* Canterbury (NZL); *Caps:* 137; *Points:* 125 (25t)

2. AARON SMITH
Age: 26; *Position:* scrum-half; *Club:* Manawatu (NZL); *Caps:* 38; *Points:* 57 (11t, 1c)

3. JULIAN SAVEA
Age: 24; *Position:* wing; *Club:* Wellington (NZL); *Caps:* 33; *Points:* 150 (30t)

4. MA'A NONU
Age: 33; *Position:* centre; *Club:* Wellington (NZL); *Caps:* 94; *Points:* 130 (26t)

5. BRODIE RETALLICK
Age: 24; *Position:* second row; *Club:* Bay of Plenty (NZL); *Caps:* 36; *Points:* 5 (1t)

Argentina

Argentina's stock has been steadily rising ever since the first Rugby World Cup 28 years ago. The team's seminal moment looked to have arrived with a superb run to the Rugby World Cup 2007 semi-finals but a modest performance in 2011 leaves Los Pumas scrambling to rejoin the elite.

Argentina
www.uar.com.ar

PLAYING STRIP Blue and white shirts, white shorts, white socks

FORM SINCE RUGBY WORLD CUP 2011

Played:	44
Won:	16
Lost:	27
Drawn:	1
Winning percentage:	37.5
Points for:	1,177
Points against:	1,126
Points scored per match:	26.7
Points conceded per match:	25.6

Biggest victory: 111-0 v Brazil at Santiago on May 23, 2012

Heaviest defeat: 73-13 v South Africa at FNB Stadium, Soweto, on Aug 17, 2013

World Rugby Ranking (at Jan 2015) 9

RUGBY WORLD CUP PERFORMANCES

1987	Pool stages
1991	Pool stages
1995	Pool stages
1999	Quarter-finals
2003	Pool stages
2007	Semi-finals
2011	Quarter-finals

Argentina have played in all seven Rugby World Cups to date but it was not until the 2007 Tournament that Los Pumas truly announced themselves on the international scene, when they reached the semi-finals and twice beat hosts France to finish third. The team's progress has been more modest than the South Americans would have hoped since that memorable performance eight years ago but recent displays have offered room for optimism again.

Reaching the Rugby World Cup's latter stages was, for a long time, no more than a pipe dream for Argentina, who recorded only one victory in their first three Tournaments and were knocked out in the pool stages on each occasion. That single success came in the inaugural 1987 competition when captain Hugo Porta kicked five penalties to help secure a 25-16 victory over Italy. Defeats by Fiji and New Zealand, though, ended the team's interest before the knockout stages, and there was disappointment again at Rugby World Cup 1991 when Los Pumas were beaten by Wales, Western Samoa and eventual champions Australia.

Victory eluded them at Rugby World Cup 1995 too but there were some signs of improvement in South Africa, where Argentina began to push their rivals closer and harder than before. They lost each of their pool matches by only six points and that potential began to bear fruit at Rugby World Cup 1999.

Despite a 23-18 defeat in their opening match against Wales at the Millennium Stadium, Argentina recorded their first Rugby World Cup win in 12 years, beating Samoa 32-16, and then overcame Japan 33-12 to book a quarter-final play-off with Ireland. In their finest victory to date, Los Pumas upset the odds in Lens with a stunning 28-24 win and, while the remarkable journey ended with defeat by France in the last eight, the seeds of future success had been sown. Fly-half Gonzalo Quesada finished as the Tournament's top-scorer with 102 points and players who went on to form the heart of the 2007 team – Mario Ledesma, Juan Martín Fernández Lobbe and Agustín Pichot – had made their mark on the world stage.

COACH

DANIEL HOURCADE

Daniel Hourcade began coaching at Universitario Rugby Club de Tucuman in 1993 before becoming head coach of the Argentina Under-21 and Sevens sides. He continued his international experience across the Atlantic with Portugal, where he worked with the Sevens and women's teams before returning to Argentina's domestic scene. Four consecutive Americas Rugby Championship titles with the Jaguars and a Vodacom Cup final with the Pampas XV firmly established Hourcade in the national frame and he was announced as Argentina's head coach in October 2013 following the resignation of Santiago Phelan.

STAR PLAYER

NICOLÁS SÁNCHEZ

Position:..Fly-half
Born:..October 26, 1988
San Miguel de Tucuman, Argentina
Club:..Toulon (Fra)
Height:.....................................1.77m (5ft 10in)
Weight:.......................................83kg (182lb)
Caps:..30
Points:....................230 (2t, 26c, 48p, 8dg)

Nicolás Sánchez was handed his Test debut in May 2010 and has long since cemented himself as Los Pumas' most distinguished and reliable performer. The small but fearless fly-half's tenacious style of play embodies the Argentine spirit, but he is also his side's creative fulcrum – shown by his place as top tackler in the 2013 Rugby Championship and highest points scorer in the 2014 Tournament. Consistent off the tee and influential out of hand, Sánchez's fitness and form will be crucial if Argentina are to trouble the latter stages in England.

PLAYERS TO WATCH

1. JUAN MARTÍN FERNÁNDEZ LOBBE
Age: 33; *Position:* No. 8; *Club:* Toulon (Fra); *Caps:* 61; *Points:* 30 (6t)

2. JUAN IMHOFF
Age: 27; *Position:* wing; *Club:* Racing Métro (Fra); *Caps:* 26; *Points:* 65 (13t)

3. AGUSTÍN CREEVY
Age: 30; *Position:* hooker; *Club:* Worcester (Eng); *Caps:* 36; *Points:* 0

4. MARCELO BOSCH
Age: 31; *Position:* centre; *Club:* Saracens (Eng); *Caps:* 33; *Points:* 45 (4t, 2c, 7p)

5. MARCOS AYERZA
Age: 32; *Position:* prop; *Club:* Leicester (Eng); *Caps:* 57; *Points:* 5 (1t)

Argentina's progress has seen them join the southern hemisphere's Rugby Championship

A difficult draw at Rugby World Cup 2003 saw Argentina's momentum stall as victories over Namibia and Romania, but defeat to Australia, left Marcelo Loffreda's side needing to beat Ireland in the final pool match to progress. Quesada kicked 12 points in a nail-biting encounter in Adelaide but it was Ireland who edged through with a 16-15 win.

At Rugby World Cup 2007, there was another tough draw for Argentina,

who were placed in the 'Pool of Death' alongside Ireland and hosts France. They faced the French in the first match of the Tournament at the Stade de France and sent shockwaves through the competition with a stunning 17-12 win. Los Pumas then proved the victory was far from a one-off, beating Georgia, Namibia and Ireland to go through to the quarter-finals as pool winners. Led by captain Pichot and

spurred on by the likes of Fernández Lobbe, the impressive run continued with a 19-13 victory over Scotland before Argentina finally lost in the semi-finals to South Africa, who went on to be crowned champions. If there was any doubt surrounding their success, Argentina proved their earlier victory had been no fluke by beating France again in the Bronze Final to confirm their place among the elite.

Their excellent result in 2007 was ultimately rewarded with a place in the Rugby Championship from 2012 but it was only in the 2014 Tournament, in their final match against Australia, that Argentina managed to record a victory. Their displays at Rugby World Cup 2011 were also tinged with disappointment as the team qualified for the last eight behind England but were convincingly beaten by the All Blacks in Auckland.

The country's traditional approach of defensive solidity built on a sturdy pack has needed adapting in recent years but there has been enough in recent performances to suggest Daniel Hourcade's side are starting to make the transition. Drawn alongside New Zealand in Pool C, Argentina are likely to be battling it out with Tonga, Georgia and Namibia for second place and progress to the knockout stages. History suggests Los Pumas will be more than up for the fight.

Tonga

Tonga are aiming to progress to the knockout rounds of a Rugby World Cup for the first time in their history when they travel to England for the 2015 edition. The 'Ikale Tahi have competed in all but one Tournament and shown a gradual improvement, with their next aim being to finally progress from their pool.

Tonga provided one of the biggest shocks of Rugby World Cup 2011 when they stunned eventual finalists France 19-14 in Wellington to announce they are a side that are not to be taken lightly. But for a surprise 25-20 defeat by Canada and a bit of luck, Tonga would have replaced the off-colour Europeans in the quarter-finals. The statement of intent fell short though, as the victory over France came in their final pool match and that, along with a resounding 31-18 win against Japan, was not enough to progress after they had already recorded a defeat against hosts New Zealand. The French and eventual champions New Zealand moved into the last eight and Tonga were left to reflect on what might have been.

It has not always been so close to the wire for Tonga as, at Rugby World Cup 1987, the Pacific Islanders finished bottom of Pool Two after failing to win any of their games. Defeats by Canada, Wales and Ireland put paid to their inaugural Tournament in quick style.

Four years later Tonga did not qualify and they only showed a minor improvement at Rugby World Cup 1995 in South Africa, with one victory in their pool against Ivory Coast. The match was overshadowed by an injury to Ivory Coast's Max Brito, who damaged the fourth and fifth vertebrae in his neck during a tackle and was subsequently left paralysed for life. After defeats by France and Scotland, Tonga finished third in their pool, an improvement on their first Tournament but still not enough to reach the knockout stages.

Rugby World Cup 1999 was the first to be held in the professional era and Tonga claimed their first major scalp when they defeated Italy 28-25. While Italy had not yet joined what is now the Six Nations, they were only months away from doing so and Tonga's victory over the Azzurri marked an important chapter in their presence on the world stage, with the win at Leicester's Welford Road secured by a side which included Tongan greats Epi Taione, Sililo Martens and Sateki Tuipulotu. Despite that result, the 'Ikale Tahi were unable to progress from their pool yet again as they were swept aside in their other two pool matches. The first saw them dismissed by New Zealand 45-9 but there was much worse to come as England ran in 13 tries and swept them aside in a 101-10 victory at Twickenham.

Rugby World Cup 2003 can be considered as Tonga's lowest point in

COACH

MANA OTAI

Former Auckland flanker Mana Otai made five Test appearances for Tonga and was captain at Rugby World Cup 1995, scoring a try in the victory over Ivory Coast. He took over as head coach of the national team in September 2012 in place of Toutai Kefu, who had been in temporary charge. Under Otai, 'Ikale Tahi have continued to play their heady mix of strong scrummaging and attacking flair and their results have ensured they continue to hold a position just outside the top 10 of the World Rugby Rankings.

Tonga
www.tongarugbyunion.net

PLAYING STRIP Red shirts, white shorts, red socks

FORM SINCE RUGBY WORLD CUP 2011

Played:	18
Won:	7
Lost:	10
Drawn:	1
Winning percentage:	41.66%
Points for:	371
Points against:	416
Points scored per match:	20.61
Points conceded per match:	23.11

Biggest victory: 40-12 v United States in Gloucester on November 15, 2014

Heaviest defeat: 45-17 v Fiji in Lautoka on June 14, 2014

World Rugby Ranking (at Jan 2015): 13

RUGBY WORLD CUP PERFORMANCES

1987	Pool stages
1991	Did not qualify
1995	Pool stages
1999	Pool stages
2003	Pool stages
2007	Pool stages
2011	Pool stages

STAR PLAYER

SONA TAUMALOLO

Position:..Prop
Born:............November 13, 1981, Ha'akame, Tonga
Club:..Racing Métro (Fra)
Height: 1.85m (6ft 1in)
Weight: 112kg (247lbs)
Caps: 13
Points:..20 (4t)

Sona Taumalolo has both the experience and guile to lead Tonga in the forwards battle in a demanding pool which contains four physical sides in defending champions New Zealand, Argentina, Georgia and Namibia. A veteran of Rugby World Cup 2011, Taumalolo scored a try against New Zealand in the 41-10 defeat and has experience of both southern and northern hemisphere Rugby. The 33-year-old, who has played for Super Rugby side the Chiefs and in France for Perpignan and more recently Racing Métro, is a strong ball-carrier who enjoys work in the loose.

the history of the Tournament as they failed to build on their previous progress and slumped to four defeats in their pool. They began their campaign with a 36-12 defeat by Italy and, although they pushed Wales all the way in a 27-20 loss, things went from bad to worse in a 91-7 loss to New Zealand before Tonga rounded off their competition with another defeat, this time 24-7 to Canada.

Arguably, this lowest ebb provided a catalyst for change and by Rugby World Cup 2007, Tonga had assembled their strongest line-up to date with lock Viliami Vaki, back-row forward Hale T-Pole, number 8 Finau Maka and flanker Nili Latu in the squad –genuine world-class competitors who gave Tonga an edge they had never had before.

Latu went on to be included in *The Independent's* list of the 50 Best Rugby Players in the World a year later and the new strength showed as Tonga began

the Tournament with a convincing 25-15 win over the United States before they brought to an end their nine-game losing run against Samoa with a 19-15 victory.

With the knockout stages still within their sights, Tonga went into their next game against South Africa knowing that victory would be enough to see them over the line. An epic match ensued against the world champions-elect, with Tonga taking a 10-7 lead early in the second half when prop Kisi Pulu was driven over. Nerves were jangling for the Springboks but they hit back to overhaul the 'Ikale Tahi and record a hard-fought 30-25 victory. It meant Tonga had to win their last pool game against a Martin Corry-led England and, while they started strongly and moved into a 10-3 lead, the boot of Jonny Wilkinson saw England triumph 36-20 in Paris.

That brings us back to 2011 and the scene of Tonga's biggest Rugby World Cup scalp to date – that of France – and a year later they also defeated Scotland 21-15 in Aberdeen.

Tonga have since climbed the World Rugby Rankings to 13th place – leapfrogging Italy in the process – and will be hoping that Rugby World Cup 2015 in England is their time to advance to the latter stages of the competition for the first time.

PLAYERS TO WATCH

1. STEVE MAFI
Age: 25; *Position:* flanker; *Club:* Leicester (Eng); *Caps:* 10; *Points:* 0
2. VILIAMI FIHAKI
Age: 28; *Position:* No. 8; *Club:* Sale (Eng);*Caps:* 5; *Points:* 10 (2t)
3. LATIUME FOSITA
Age: 22; *Position:* fly-half; *Club:* Northland (NZL); *Caps:* 8; *Points:* 29 (7c, 5p)
4. WILLIAM HELU
Age: 29; *Position:* wing/centre; *Club:* Wasps (Eng); *Caps:* 19; *Points:* 30 (6t)
5. LISIATE FA'AOSO
Age: 32; *Position:* lock; *Club:* Agen (Fra); *Caps:* 16; *Points:* 5 (1t)

Tonga are bidding to reach the knockout stages for the first time in 2015

Georgia

Georgia have been the dominant force in non-Six Nations European Rugby for a decade now, and as they head to England they will be spurred on by memories of their agonising near-miss against Ireland in 2007 as they look to mark their fourth successive Rugby World Cup appearance with a significant upset.

Georgia
www.rugby.ge

PLAYING STRIP White shirts with red trim, white shorts, red socks

FORM SINCE RUGBY WORLD CUP 2011

Played:	32
Won:	19
Lost:	12
Drawn:	1
Winning percentage:	60.93%
Points for:	765
Points against:	543
Points scored per match:	23.9
Points conceded per match:	16.9
Biggest victory:	46-0 v Russia in Tbilisi on March 17, 2012
Heaviest defeat:	49-7 v Ireland in Dublin on November 16, 2014
World Rugby Ranking (at Jan 2015)	15

RUGBY WORLD CUP PERFORMANCES

1987	Did not enter
1991	Did not enter
1995	Did not qualify
1999	Did not qualify
2003	Pool stages
2007	Pool stages
2011	Pool stages

When Giorgi Shkinin intercepted a stray pass from Ireland's Peter Stringer and stormed 70 yards to touch down at the Stade Chaban-Delmas in Bordeaux on September 17, 2007, it was a signal that Georgian Rugby had finally arrived on the world stage.

Malkhaz Tcheishvili's men had entered Rugby World Cup 2007 as relative also-rans having qualified by virtue of finishing second in the European Nations Cup behind Romania, but the way they pushed Ireland to the limit ended any notion of Georgia being there merely to make up the numbers.

All the nation's exploits since have been measured against that night when they came so close to one of the biggest upsets in Rugby World Cup history, edging into a second-half lead before Ireland, the Pool D favourites, eventually battled to a nail-biting 14-10 success. Georgia have continued to build steadily on that success, winning six of the last seven European Nations Cup tournaments, the continent's second-tier international competition behind the Six Nations, which qualified them for Rugby World Cup 2015 as of right.

Rugby has been an established and hugely popular sport in Georgia since its domestic league was founded in 1961, with the Georgian Rugby Union established three years later. The majority of its first three decades were played in the shadow of the USSR, who picked its best players for international fixtures.

Following independence in 1991, Georgia became members of World Rugby and narrowly failed to qualify for Rugby World Cup 1999 after losing a two-legged play-off against Tonga, despite a narrow second-leg win in Tbilisi.

Georgia's first European Nations Cup title arrived in 2001, bolstering hopes of qualification for the 2003 showpiece, and a year later the Georgians would get their chance with only old rivals Russia standing in the way of a first appearance in the Tournament. With the winners guaranteed qualification and the losers set for a play-off, a crowd of almost 50,000 in Tbilisi saw Georgia come from behind to beat Russia 17-13 and make it to Rugby World Cup for the first time. Despite heavy defeats to England, South Africa and Samoa, Georgia's final pool match

COACH

MILTON HAIG

New Zealander Milton Haig was appointed as Georgia's head coach in 2011 following the departure of former Scotland coach Richie Dixon. Georgia wanted a Kiwi to take charge and asked the New Zealand Rugby Union for advice on possible candidates. Haig had a brief playing career with Southland in the National Provincial Championship before going on to coach Bay of Plenty then Counties Manukau for four seasons. Haig had also worked with the New Zealand Under-20 side and showed no hesitation in accepting the Georgia post in January 2012.

improvement. Georgia only went down 15-6 to Scotland, beat long-time European Nations Cup rivals Romania 25-9, and led Argentina at half-time before falling 25-7. Even Georgia's 41-10 loss to England had a degree of respectability about it, having lost 84-6 to the same opponents on their Rugby World Cup debut eight years previously.

Georgia head into Rugby World Cup 2015 in good heart, having won nine of their last 10 matches in the European Nations Cup, the only blot a 9-9 draw against Romania in Bucharest in March 2013. And in November 2013, they managed another breakthrough when they held on for a nail-biting 16-15 win over Samoa in Tbilisi, arguably eclipsing their performance against Ireland as the most notable performance in the nation's Rugby history. Georgian Rugby Union president Giorgi Nijaradze emerged from raucous scenes of celebration to say: "Today was a miracle and Georgia played sensationally. I have never seen such creative play from us."

But with success comes expectation. No longer the plucky minnows, Georgia will expect to see off both Tonga and Namibia in Pool C, avoid an embarrassment against the mighty All Blacks while the clash with Argentina could prove decisive.

Georgia have made the European Nations Cup their own property in recent years

against Uruguay offered them an ideal opportunity to end their first RWC appearance with a win but a 24-12 score in favour of the South Americans ensured Georgia's first experience of the biggest stage was to be a disappointing one.

Four years later, Georgia were back and their heroic performance against Ireland was tinged only by a feeling that it might have been even better. Merab Kvirikashvili missed a penalty and four drop goals, and a late try attempt was ruled out after a video replay. Despite defeats to Argentina and France, Georgia at least left the Tournament on a high having convincingly beaten Namibia 30-0 to get their first Rugby World Cup victory on the board.

The next Rugby World Cup in 2011 indicated plenty of further

Namibia

Namibia will be looking to win a Rugby World Cup match for the first time in 2015, despite qualifying for every Tournament since 1999. The transition to Rugby at the very highest level has been hard for the Welwitschias, but hopes are high they have learned their lesson and are ready to do more than make up the numbers.

Namibia

www.namibianrugby.com

PLAYING STRIP Blue shirts, white shorts, blue socks

FORM SINCE RUGBY WORLD CUP 2011

Played:	14
Won:	9
Lost:	5
Drawn:	0
Winning percentage:	64.28%
Points for:	544
Points against:	357
Points scored per match:	38.86
Points conceded per match:	25.5
Biggest victory:	89-10 v Madagascar in Antananarivo on July 6, 2014
Heaviest defeat:	29-20 v Portugal in Lisbon on November 22, 2014
World Rugby Ranking (at Jan 2015)	23

RUGBY WORLD CUP PERFORMANCES

1987	Did not enter
1991	Did not enter
1995	Did not qualify
1999	Pool stages
2003	Pool stages
2007	Pool stages
2011	Pool stages

Over the course of Namibia's 15 previous Rugby World Cup matches they have shipped a total of 974 points, with 60 per cent of their opponents racking up a score of at least 50 against them. They also slumped to the worst defeat in RWC history 12 years ago when they were beaten 142-0 by Australia. There is no hiding that those statistics make for grim reading but,

unlike many of the lower-ranked nations involved in this year's showpiece, they have savoured victory against one of the big boys in the past.

In 1991, a year after the Namibian Rugby Union was formed, they enjoyed a 2-0 series win over a touring Ireland side. The series, which saw Richard Wallace make his debut for the Irish, was sealed with Namibia running in an impressive five tries to win 26-15 in the second match after clinching the first 15-6. Namibia's introduction as an independent Rugby nation was too late for them to take part in Rugby World Cup 1991 and they just missed out on qualification for Rugby World Cup 1995 in South Africa four years later.

When they finally secured their place at the top table in 1999, Fiji took only 40 minutes to expose them to the harsh realities of competing with the best as they ran in six tries and took a 43-6 lead at the break in Beziers, France. Although Heino Senekal touched down Namibia's first RWC try in the second half, they still slipped to a 67-18 defeat. France (47-13) and Canada (72-11) also made light work of the Welwitschias, but Namibia captain Quin Hough's second-half try against the Canadians at least ensured they crossed the whitewash in all of their matches — something eight other nations had failed to do.

After a chastening maiden experience, Namibia returned for more at Rugby World Cup 2003 but, if anything, it was even harder for them second time around. Once

again they lost all their matches, but they hit their lowest ebb when Australia ran in 22 unanswered tries — with Chris Latham grabbing five — on their way to a 142-0 triumph. That remains the worst defeat ever suffered by any side at a Rugby World Cup as woeful tackling gave the Wallabies free rein to run riot in Adelaide.

Bolstered by the presence of a young Jacques Burger, Namibia enjoyed their best Rugby World Cup moment so far in 2007, when they gave Eddie O'Sullivan's Ireland a real scare. The Irish raced into a 27-3 lead after 59 minutes but Namibia rallied and came back to within 10 points before Ireland

COACH

DANIE VERMEULEN

The 39-year-old will become the first national coach in Rugby World Cup history to fulfil his duties from a wheelchair. Vermeulen, who was a prop for the Cats — now the Lions — in Super 12, had his own playing career cut short when he was paralysed in a car crash in 2000. Prior to that he had been earmarked as the next big thing for Namibian Rugby, but hopes are high he can now live up to that tag as head coach. He has engineered a strong team spirit within the Namibian squad, which secured qualification against the odds.

STAR PLAYER

JACQUES BURGER

Position:	Back row
Born:	July 29, 1983 , Windhoek, Namibia
Club:	Saracens (Eng)
Height:	1.88m (6ft 2in)
Weight:	106kg (234lb)
Caps:	30
Points:	25 (5t)

The tough-tackling Saracens flanker has a fierce reputation and was named in the top five performers at Rugby World Cup 2011 by the Tournament News Service. Although Namibia struggled in New Zealand, Burger's commitment was praised as he completed 64 tackles in their four matches. His talismanic defensive displays also epitomise Sarries' 'Wolf-Pack' mentality; he made a record-breaking 37 successful hits against Exeter in the Premiership in November 2013. Tackling is an art form to Jacques Burger and he is a master of his craft who can hold his own against the world's elite.

who had recently joined Saracens at the time, was praised for the way he led by example and put his body on the line for a losing cause. He was even included in the top five performers at the Tournament by the Rugby News Service. Burger's involvement for his country since that Tournament has been limited by injury and club commitments, but his stellar form for Saracens has won him even more plaudits in recent years – the biggest example being his key role in the dismantling of Clermont in the Heineken Cup last year.

In his absence, Namibia looked set to miss out on qualification for Rugby World Cup 2015 before clinching their place in dramatic fashion. They went into their last game against Madagascar needing a substantial 53-point winning margin to pip Zimbabwe, but they need not have worried as they ran in 13 tries in total to win 89-10. Renaldo Bothma bagged four of them as Namibia outclassed the Madagascans to become the second African side at the Tournament.

Danie Vermeulen's side were rewarded with a place in Pool C and they face the toughest possible start to their 2015 campaign as they take on the might of New Zealand at the Olympic Stadium on September 24. Aside from the All Blacks, Namibia will also lock horns with Argentina, Tonga and Georgia, who perhaps present the best opportunity for the Welwitschias to break their Rugby World Cup hoodoo.

scored again to win 32-17. Despite that stirring effort, it was a depressing case of déjà vu for the Welwitschias, with France securing their biggest ever win by beating them 87-10 and Argentina also winning comfortably 63-3. The campaign ended with a disappointing 30-0 loss to Georgia, who they will meet again in this year's competition.

Under the stewardship of Johan Diergaardt, with Burger now skipper, Namibia once again failed to break their duck at Rugby World Cup 2011 in New Zealand. They were well beaten by South Africa (87-0) and Wales (81-7), while they were also unable to topple Fiji (49-25) and Samoa (49-12).

Despite Namibia's woes, Burger managed to catch the eye and enhance his growing reputation. The flanker,

PLAYERS TO WATCH

1. RENALDO BOTHMA
Age: 25; *Position:* back row; *Club:* Pumas (RSA); *Caps:* 3; *Points:* 25 (5t)

2. TINUS DU PLESSIS
Age: 31; *Position:* back row; *Club:* Wanderers (Nam); *Caps:* 39; *Points:* 25 (5t)

3 CHRYSANDER BOTHA
Age: 26; *Position:* full-back; *Club:* Exeter (Eng); *Caps:* 29; *Points:* 142 (15t, 14c, 13p)

4 THEUNS KOTZE
Age: 27; *Position:* fly-half; *Club:* Bourg-en-Bresse (Fra); *Caps:* 19; *Points:* 226 (2t, 48c, 35p, 5dg)

5 TJIUEE UANIVI
Age: 24; *Position:* lock; *Club:* Brive (Fra); *Caps:* 0; *Points:* 0

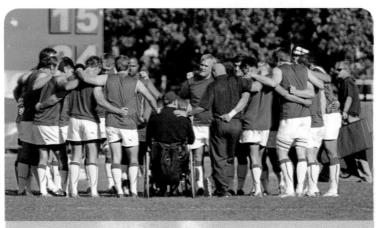

Rugby World Cup has been an unremitting struggle so far for Namibia

ALLEZ FRANCE AS ALL BLACKS SHOCKED
OCTOBER 31, 1999, TWICKENHAM, LONDON

The 1999 semi-final between France and New Zealand at Twickenham must rank as the greatest match in Rugby World Cup history. France were never given a hope in the build-up against an All Blacks side that were huge favourites to lift the Webb Ellis Cup after losing the Final four years earlier. New Zealand lived up to their favourites' tag by taking a 24-10 lead with the unstoppable Jonah Lomu scoring twice but France, inspired by the kicking and attacking play of Christophe Lamaison, stormed back in incredible fashion. Lamaison scored 28 points, including the first try, and breathtaking second-half tries from Christian Dominici, Richard Dourthe and Philippe Bernat-Salles sent France to a Final which they eventually lost to Australia.

France players celebrate after their amazing second-half comeback at Twickenham

France

France's Rugby World Cup history glitters with glorious victories, but Les Bleus have yet to win the one game that really matters, the Final itself. Famous for playing with élan and panache, France possess some of the world's most potent backs, supported by fine forwards.

Jacques Fouroux's France travelled to Australia and New Zealand in 1987 for the inaugural Rugby World Cup confident after enjoying a Grand Slam-winning Five Nations campaign.

A 20-20 draw with Scotland got France's campaign off to a stuttering start but they beat Romania (55-12) and Zimbabwe (70-12) to top their pool. After dispatching Fiji 31-16 in the quarter-finals, France played co-hosts Australia in the semi-finals in Sydney. With the scores level at 24-24 late on, France

full-back Serge Blanco finished a move involving 11 team-mates which is often referred to as the finest try in Rugby World Cup history. Fouroux's men never got going in the Final, however, with the All Blacks sealing a 29-9 victory.

France co-hosted the 1991 Tournament, but endured their most disappointing Rugby World Cup to date. Under the stewardship of Daniel Dubroca, unconvincing victories over Romania (30-3), Fiji (33-9) and Canada (19-13) ensued before they were outclassed by eventual runners-up England in a one-sided quarter-final.

France arrived in South Africa for Rugby World Cup 1995 with Pierre Berbizier at the helm and breezed through pool matches against Scotland (22-19), Tonga (38-10) and Ivory Coast (54-18) to set up a quarter-final showdown with Ireland. A 26-point haul from fly-half Thierry Lacroix sealed a 36-12 success for Les Bleus but they were undone by South Africa No.10 Joel Stransky in the semi-finals as the Springboks edged to a 19-15 triumph. France beat England 19-9 in the third-place play-off.

Following a last-place Five Nations finish, Jean-Claude Skrela's side recouped some much-needed confidence at Rugby World Cup 1999 with pool-stage wins over Canada (33-20), Namibia (47-13) and Fiji (28-19), before a 47-26 quarter-final triumph over Argentina. What followed was arguably the greatest comeback in Rugby history as, trailing 24-10 shortly after half-time, France fought

back to secure a 43-31 victory over a stunned All Blacks side. Sadly for France, they could not replicate their semi-final heroics in the Final as Australia ran out 35-12 winners in Cardiff.

Rugby World Cup 2003 was held in Australia and free-scoring France beat Fiji (61-18), Japan (51-29), Scotland (51-9) and United States (41-14) in the pool matches. Ireland lay in wait in the quarter-finals, and Bernard Laporte's men cruised to a 43-21 victory. France came up against England in the semi-finals and bowed out to the eventual winners 24-7, before losing to New Zealand 40-13 in the third-place play-off.

COACH

PHILIPPE SAINT-ANDRÉ

A skilful winger in his playing days, Philippe Saint-André was offered the chance to coach France in 2007 but he declined the role when the French Rugby Federation refused to hire Laurent Seigne to his backroom staff. Saint-André instead remained as director of Rugby at Sale before taking the sporting president's role at Toulon a year later and playing an important role in their subsequent domestic and European dominance. Four years later Saint-Andre finally answered France's call, succeeding Marc Lièvremont after Rugby World Cup 2011. It has not been plain sailing, with two fourth-place Six Nations finishes either side of their wooden spoon disappointment in 2013.

France
www.ffr.fr

PLAYING STRIP Blue shirts, white collar, Tricolore shoulder stripes, blue shorts, red socks

FORM SINCE RUGBY WORLD CUP 2011

Played:	32
Won:	13
Lost:	17
Drawn:	2
Winning percentage:	43.75%
Points for:	645
Points against:	646
Points scored per match:	20.16
Points conceded per match:	20.19
Biggest victory:	49-10, v Argentina in Tucuman, on June 23, 2012
Heaviest defeat:	30-0, v New Zealand in Christchurch on June 15, 2013
World Rugby Ranking (at Jan 2015)	7

RUGBY WORLD CUP PERFORMANCES

1987	Runners-up
1991	Quarter-finals
1995	Semi-finals
1999	Runners-up
2003	Semi-finals
2007	Semi-finals
2011	Runners-up

STAR PLAYER

THIERRY DUSAUTOIR

Position:	Flanker and captain
Born:	November 18, 1981, Abidjan, Ivory Coast
Club:	Toulouse (Fra)
Height:	1.88m (6ft 2in)
Weight:	100kg (220lb)
Caps:	70
Points:	30 (6t)

Ivory Coast-born Thierry Dusautoir was a latecomer to Rugby, taking up the sport aged 16 after his parents moved to France. He made his club debut for Bordeaux in 2001 before moving to Biarritz in 2004, and scored a try on his France debut in 2006. A move to Toulouse followed and Dusautoir shone against New Zealand at Rugby World Cup 2007. He was named captain in 2009 and led them to a Six Nations Grand Slam the following year. Dusautoir helped France to the brink of Rugby World Cup 2011 glory and he was named World Rugby Player of the Year, but the team has faltered in his injury-enforced absence more recently.

France pipped England to host Rugby World Cup 2007 but Les Bleus fell to a 17-12 loss to Argentina in their opening match. France recovered to qualify for the knockout stages courtesy of victories over Georgia (64-7), Namibia (87-10) and Ireland (25-3). Les Bleus were pitted against New Zealand for the fourth time in Rugby World Cup history and once again they proved to be the All Blacks' bogey side by clinching a 20-18

quarter-final victory. The scene was set for a red, white and blue march to the Paris Final but it was not to be France's day as England ground out a 14-9 semi-final victory before losing to South Africa in the Final. France lost 34-10 to Argentina in the Bronze Final.

Marc Lièvremont inherited the coaching reins from Bernard Laporte in 2007 and, after his early tenure was marred by embarrassing defeats,

few Rugby pundits tipped France to excel at Rugby World Cup 2011 in New Zealand. That view was backed up when, following victories over Japan (47-21) and Canada (46-19) and a 37-17 loss to New Zealand, France slipped to a 19-14 defeat to Tonga and only qualified for the quarter-finals by the skin of their teeth. France raised their game to overcome England 19-12 in the quarter-finals and edged Warren Gatland's high-flying Wales 9-8 in the semi-finals to set up a repeat of the 1987 Final against the All Blacks. A routine victory was expected for Graham Henry's side but it was anything but for the All Blacks. A converted try from Thierry Dusautoir saw France fight back from 8-0 down to trail 8-7 with half an hour remaining but a missed penalty by Francois Trinh-Duc 15 minutes from time meant the All Blacks clung on for victory.

Philippe Saint-André assumed control of France following Rugby World Cup 2011 and he has not fared much better than his predecessor. His first Six Nations campaign at the helm in 2012 ended with a fourth-place finish, but the 2013 campaign was a colossal failure as France collected the wooden spoon after defeats to Italy, Wales and England. Victories over England, Italy and Scotland in the 2014 campaign led to a fourth-place finish, offering hope that France have an outside chance of landing Rugby's ultimate prize in enemy territory in 2015.

PLAYERS TO WATCH

1. MATHIEU BASTAREAUD
Age: 26; *Position:* centre; *Club:* Toulon (Fra); *Caps:* 28; *Points:* 10 (2t)
2. WESLEY FOFANA
Age: 27; *Position:* centre/wing; *Club:* Clermont Auvergne (Fra); *Caps:* 30; *Points:* 55 (11t)
3. YOANN HUGET
Age: 28; *Position:* wing; *Club:* Toulouse (Fra); *Caps:* 33; *Points:* 30 (6t)
4. PASCAL PAPE
Age: 34; *Position:* lock; *Club:* Stade Français (Fra); *Caps:* 57; *Points:* 20 (4t)
5. JULES PLISSON
Age: 23; *Position:* fly-half; *Club:* Stade Français (Fra); *Caps:* 4; *Points:* 3 (1p)

France show their pain after losing the Rugby World Cup 2011 Final to New Zealand

POOL D

Ireland

A meticulous coach and a home-bound hero will pull Ireland's Rugby World Cup strings. Kiwi boss Joe Schmidt and fly-half Jonathan Sexton will aim to drive the Irish to their best-ever global showing in England as they look to finally get beyond the quarter-finals.

Ireland's pride in punching above their weight on the international stage remains tempered by a nagging Rugby World Cup feeling. The Irish boast only six per cent of England's countrywide player base, yet continue to hold their own in the world arena.

Five quarter-finals in seven Tournaments is hardly a shabby return for an island nation claiming only 153,000 registered players across all levels. Yet such an achievement still baffles and frustrates in almost equal measure: once positioned in the knockout stages, the Irish have been unable to strike. And it is this failure to

kick on that rankles and irks the backs of minds from Dublin to Donegal.

Ireland's failure to progress past Pool D at Rugby World Cup 2007 ultimately led to coach Eddie O'Sullivan's exit after the following Six Nations. So when Ireland beat two-time champions Australia en route to topping Pool C at Rugby World Cup 2011, hopes were higher than ever that Declan Kidney's men could reach their first-ever semi-final. Instead they ran headfirst into Pool D runners-up Wales, who had sneaked through a horror-show line-up including South Africa and the potent Samoa in New Zealand. Leinster's second Heineken Cup victory in three years had reverberated across the summer, following Munster's two European club victories in 2006 and 2008. European club dominance was increasingly feeding into international confidence for the Irish, with the 2009 Grand Slam still in memory too. For the likes of world power Brian O'Driscoll, the Tournament in New Zealand offered a tantalising chance to crown his glittering career in new glory.

Instead flanker Sam Warburton's inspired breakdown work stymied Ireland at every turn, depriving O'Driscoll and his backline of any rhythm. Ireland's monster back row of Stephen Ferris, Sean O'Brien and Jamie Heaslip were outgunned by Warburton, Dan Lydiate and Taulupe Faletau. The Irish lost out 22-10, while Wales were trumped 9-8 by France in the semi-finals.

Ireland's 12-month build-up to Rugby World Cup 2015 was billed as the scramble to secure O'Driscoll's long-term successor in the

COACH

JOE SCHMIDT

Among the most cerebral coaches in world Rugby, the tireless thinker demands ever-higher standards of his players and staff. Renowned for short, sharp training sessions with peerless expectations, New Zealander Schmidt challenges his players to prepare as much mentally for midweek practice as match-day action. After club success with Clermont and Leinster, now the former teacher is eyeing new ground with Ireland's national team.

number 13 shirt. Just as crucial though, was the continuing development of meticulous boss Joe Schmidt's gameplan. Kiwi mastermind Schmidt was the coaching cornerstone of Leinster's rise to European dominance, and that after a highly impressive stint at Clermont. One of the game's great lateral thinkers, Schmidt's taskmaster style pushed Ireland to new levels of accuracy and skill in claiming the 2014 Six Nations, the title sealed in O'Driscoll's international farewell.

Transferring that success to the global summit remains an altogether different challenge however: not least as Ireland

Ireland

www.irishrugby.ie

PLAYING STRIP Green shirts with white trim, white shorts, green socks

FORM SINCE RUGBY WORLD CUP 2011

Played:	30
Won:	16
Lost:	12
Drawn:	2
Winning percentage:	56.66%
Points for:	700
Points against:	558
Points scored per match:	23.33
Points conceded per match:	18.6
Biggest victory:	49-7 v Georgia at Aviva Stadium on November 16, 2014
Heaviest defeat:	60-0 v New Zealand at Waikato Stadium on June 23, 2012
World Rugby Ranking (at Jan 2015)	3

RUGBY WORLD CUP PERFORMANCES

1987	Quarter-finals
1991	Quarter-finals
1995	Quarter-finals
1999	Quarter-final play-offs
2003	Quarter-finals
2007	Pool stages
2011	Quarter-finals

STAR PLAYER

JONATHAN SEXTON

Position:	Fly-half
Born:	July 11, 1985, Dublin, Ireland
Club:	Racing Métro (Fra)
Height:	1.83m (6ft 2in)
Weight:	92kg (202lb)
Caps:	47
Points:	423 (8t, 49c, 93p, 2dg)

The prodigal half-back's French revolution is over and Ireland can plan his Rugby World Cup preparations without any interference. Jonathan Sexton's two-year Racing Métro experiment caused Ireland's coaches untold headaches over availability and fitness, losing control over the frequency of his club action. The Leinster academy graduate struggled to settle into the Parisian way of life, and Ireland's chances are boosted by his return. Now Brian O'Driscoll has departed, Ireland draw heavily on Sexton to provide attacking rhythm.

remain without a win over reigning world champions New Zealand, although both Australia and South Africa were beaten in 2014. Schmidt's men ran the All Blacks closer than ever in a 24-22 Dublin defeat in November 2013, the visitors sneaking out of jail thanks to a final-play converted try. Measured progress under Schmidt will raise hopes Ireland can finally break new Rugby World Cup ground, but history's path remains littered with pitfalls. A 13-6 defeat to Wales in Ireland's first Rugby World Cup match in 1987 led to a second-place Pool Two finish. Comfortable victories over Canada

and Tonga teed up a quarter-final clash with Australia, but the Wallabies coasted through 33-15 in Sydney. At Rugby World Cup 1991 in England that pattern was to repeat itself, as Ireland finished second in Pool B behind Scotland and the stage was set for a Lansdowne Road rematch with Australia. The return contest four years on was far closer, so much so that Ireland led 18-15 with only six minutes left on the clock. Gordon Hamilton's try had Ireland eyeing an unlikely semi-final with then champions New Zealand, only for Michael Lynagh to save Wallaby blushes and the favourites progressed

19-18 on their way to their first Rugby World Cup triumph, seeing off hosts England in the Final.

A 24-23 victory over Wales in South Africa at Rugby World Cup 1995 ensured another second-place pool finish, Ireland finishing behind Pool C winners New Zealand to make the last eight. Philippe Saint-André and Emile Ntamack scored tries in a 36-12 win, though, putting France into the semi-finals at Ireland's expense.

Ireland emerged from Pool Five at Rugby World Cup 1999, only to fall foul of a format change, losing a quarter-final play-off 28-24 to Argentina. Australia edged home 17-16 in an engaging Rugby World Cup 2003 clash in Melbourne that consigned Ireland to second place in Pool A, so while Australia eased past Scotland in their quarter-final, Ireland lost 43-21 to France.

Defeats to Argentina and hosts France at Rugby World Cup 2007 consigned Ireland to their worst-ever Rugby World Cup return, O'Sullivan's side failing to progress from Pool D. Ireland finally topped Pool C at Rugby World Cup 2011, beating Australia to boot along the way, only to run out of steam against Warburton and Wales.

France will be Ireland's main Pool D rivals on paper this time, with Italy, Canada and Romania falling in behind. Ireland's clash against Les Bleus at the Millennium Stadium to close the pool could well prove the decider.

Irish players celebrate their win over Italy at Rugby World Cup 2011

PLAYERS TO WATCH

1. CONOR MURRAY
Age: 26; *Position:* scrum-half; *Club:* Munster (Ire); *Caps:* 30; *Points:* 10 (2t)

2. PAUL O'CONNELL
Age: 35; *Position:* lock; *Club:* Munster (Ire); *Caps:* 96; *Points:* 30 (6t)

3. CIAN HEALY
Age: 27; *Position:* prop; *Club:* Leinster (Ire); *Caps:* 47; *Points:* 15 (3t)

4. SEAN O'BRIEN
Age: 28; *Position:* back row; *Club:* Leinster (Ire); *Caps:* 30; *Points:* 15 (3t)

5. PETER O'MAHONY
Age: 25; *Position:* back row; *Club:* Munster (Ire); *Caps:* 25; *Points:* 5 (1t)

Italy

Italy will compete in their eighth Rugby World Cup in England with one aim: to reach the quarter-finals for the first time. Coach Jacques Brunel has embraced that challenge and will rely on the experience and leadership of one of the Game's leading lights in Sergio Parisse.

Italy
www.federugby.it

PLAYING STRIP Light blue shirts, light blue shorts, light blue socks

FORM SINCE RUGBY WORLD CUP 2011

Played:	33
Won:	8
Lost:	25
Drawn:	0
Winning percentage:	24.24
Points for:	530
Points against:	888
Points scored per match:	16.06
Points conceded per match:	29.90
Biggest victory:	30-10 v United States in Houston on June 23, 2012
Heaviest defeat:	52-11 v England in Rome on March 15, 2014
World Rugby Ranking (at Jan 2015)	14

RUGBY WORLD CUP PERFORMANCES

1987	Pool stages
1991	Pool stages
1995	Pool stages
1999	Pool stages
2003	Pool stages
2007	Pool stages
2011	Pool stages

Italy have been an ever-present at the Rugby World Cup but have struggled to consistently match the leading nations and are now aiming to reach the latter stages of the competition for the first time. They took part in the inaugural Rugby World Cup in New Zealand in 1987 but lost their opening two games to the co-hosts and Argentina before edging to an 18-15 victory against Fiji. It was not enough to progress though, with Fiji scraping through to the next round by virtue of scoring more tries.

COACH

JACQUES BRUNEL

Jacques Brunel was a full-back for Grenoble, Carcassonne and Auch Gers before ending his nine-year playing career in 1988. He guided his former club Auch for seven seasons but made a name for himself as a coach at Club Colomiers, leading them to European Challenge Cup glory in 1998 and repeating the feat two years later at Pau. He coached the forwards in the French national team for six years, starting in 2001 when Bernard Laporte was head coach, before leaving to guide Perpignan to the French Top 14 title in the 2008/09 campaign. Brunel left Perpignan in 2012 and later that year was appointed Nick Mallett's successor as Italy coach.

The participation on the big stage fuelled the hunger for Rugby success back in Italy, where there was tremendous growth in the sport. The country reached out to experienced foreign coaches, including South Africa's Nelie Smith and Frenchmen Bertrand Fourcade and Georges Coste, and benefited from their involvement. Talented players also arrived from abroad to add a new dimension to the Italian championship. The likes of All Blacks star John Kirwan, Springbok Naas Botha and Australia's Michael Lynagh increased standards and raised the profile of Rugby in Italy.

As for the national team, the Azzurri put on brave performances in the next two Rugby World Cups, winning one game in each. In 1996, former Italy manager Giancarlo Dondi replaced Maurizio Mondelli as president of the Italian Rugby Federation and the Game continued to build momentum.

Historic results followed soon after under Coste, who had taken over the national team in 1993. The Azzurri almost stunned world champions Australia in 1994 as they suffered a narrow 23-20 defeat in Brisbane. The first victory over a Home Union team was against Ireland in Treviso in 1995, while two years later the Azzurri also beat the Irish in Dublin. That was a prelude of what was to come as on March 22 1997, Italy took a huge step forward in Grenoble. The Azzurri faced a French side that had just won the Grand Slam in the Five Nations and beat them 40-32, their first triumph over Les Bleus. It put Italian Rugby on the map.

After a challenging Rugby World Cup 1999 in Europe, when Italy lost all three of their pool matches, the Azzurri appointed Brad Johnstone as coach. The New Zealander made an immediate impact as Italy won on their Six Nations debut, defeating the 1999 Five Nations champions Scotland 34-20 in Rome.

The Azzurri failed to collect any points in the next two editions of the Six Nations during a period when the squad needed rebuilding, while former New Zealand wing and Italian league

STAR PLAYER

SERGIO PARISSE

Position:....................................Number 8/captain
Born:......September 12, 1983, La Plata, Argentina
Club:......................................Stade Français (Fra)
Height:..1.96 m (6ft 5in)
Weight:.......................................112 kg (247lb)
Caps:...108
Points:...63 (12t, 1dg)

Nobody has captained Italy more times than Sergio Parisse, who has made more than a century of international appearances since his senior debut against New Zealand in 2002 at the age of 18. His Italian father was a rugby player and Parisse arrived in Italy in 2001 and quickly established himself in the first team at Treviso. He has featured in the last three Rugby World Cups and was named Italy captain in 2008, when he was also nominated for World Rugby Player of the Year. He also made the shortlist in 2013 and is the only Italian to captain the Barbarians.

A first away win in the Six Nations against Scotland plus victory in a Rome thriller with Wales secured two wins in the competition for the first time as Italy climbed to eighth place in the World Rugby Rankings, their highest position.

Rugby World Cup 2007 followed a similar theme to previous Tournaments though, with defeat to New Zealand and wins against Romania and Portugal setting up a crunch clash with Scotland which ended in an 18-16 defeat as a quarter-final place eluded them again.

Nick Mallett took over as coach, while Parisse was named captain, and a number of encouraging results in the build-up to Rugby World Cup 2011 – including victory over France – boosted confidence that they were on the verge of finally reaching the last eight. An opening defeat to Australia put the pressure on and they again fell at the final hurdle in their pool, beating Russia and the United States but then losing to Ireland to finish third yet again.

In 2012, the Azzurri began a new era under highly-experienced coach Jacques Brunel and the 2013 Six Nations campaign featured two wins for only the second time, but the momentum was lost during an injury-plagued 2014. They will need their top players to be fit and firing if their RWC 2015 campaign is to have a happier ending.

Italy have had a series of near misses in trying to reach the knockout stages

star Kirwan replaced Johnstone at the helm. Kirwan oversaw successful qualification for Rugby World Cup 2003 and Italy built on that achievement by beating Wales in the 2003 Six Nations.

At Rugby World Cup 2003, Italy followed their opening loss to the All Blacks with victories over Tonga and Canada. In their final pool game, Kirwan's side held Wales for 60 minutes before falling to a 27-15 defeat and

missing out on a quarter-final place. A disappointing autumn tour followed and Kirwan departed after a dismal 2005 Six Nations campaign.

Former France captain and ex-national team coach Pierre Berbizier took over and in his second game in charge, the Azzurri beat Argentina in Córdoba to clinch their first win on South American soil, while wins against Portugal and Russia allowed Italy to qualify for Rugby World Cup 2007.

PLAYERS TO WATCH

1. LEONARDO SARTO
Age: 23; *Position:* wing; *Club:* Zebre (Ita); *Caps:* 12; *Points:* 15 (3t)

2. MICHELE CAMPAGNARO
Age: 22; *Position:* centre; *Club:* Treviso (Ita); *Caps:* 12; *Points:* 15 (3t)

3. SIMONE FAVARO
Age: 26; *Position:* flanker; *Club:* Treviso (Ita); *Caps:* 23; *Points:* 5 (1t)

4. ALBERTO DE MARCHI
Age: 29; *Position:* prop; *Club:* Sale (Eng); *Caps:* 23; *Points:* 0

5. LEONARDO GHIRALDINI
Age: 30; *Position:* hooker; *Club:* Leicester (Eng); *Caps:* 70; *Points:* 20 (4t)

Canada

North America's Rugby powerhouses have played in all seven Rugby World Cups and reached the quarter-finals in 1991. Canada's attempts to build on that fell short as the professional era kicked in but the Canucks' continued qualification shows their established status in the sport.

Canada have Rugby World Cup pedigree, but more for their attendance than being the life and soul of the party. In 25 matches, spanning all seven editions of the Rugby World Cup so far, Canada have recorded seven wins and have regularly been plucky losers, trying to upset the elite with little success.

The first victory came at Rugby World Cup 1987 in New Zealand against Tonga and the most recent was against the South Sea Islanders at Rugby World Cup 2011 in the same country.

Canada return to the scene of their greatest Rugby World Cup moments when the 2015 edition takes place in England. Twenty-four years ago, the Canucks reached the quarter-finals, inspired by the exploits of Gareth Rees, a fly-half who plied his trade in England for the majority of his career. Rees, who played for Wasps and Harlequins, was Canada's record points scorer until James Pritchard recently surpassed his total.

Although the Final was staged at Twickenham, all of Canada's four games took place in France. Victories over Fiji and Romania, plus a narrow 19-13 loss to France, were enough to seal a last-eight place against defending champions New Zealand, and Canada pushed them close in Lille. The All Blacks won 29-13, having led 21-3 at half-time, as the North Americans staged a mini-revival, with Al Charron scoring one of their two tries.

It seemed like a seminal moment, one of the 'newer' nations – although Canada's first international was in 1932 – testing an established super power but that was the only time that the Canucks have successfully negotiated the pool stages.

Charron and Rees played in four Rugby World Cups for Canada, but the highlight was 1991. The low point for Rees came four years later when, alongside Rod Snow, he was sent off for punching against South Africa to give Canada the ignominy of

being the only team to have more than one man sent off in a Rugby World Cup match. The Canadians lead the sending-off statistics with three, alongside Tonga, after Dan Baugh's dismissal for stamping at Rugby World Cup 1999.

The inaugural edition of Rugby World Cup in 1987 saw Canada beat Tonga, but then lose heavily to Ireland and Wales to go out. At Rugby World Cup 1995, after the high of 1991, came another victory over Romania, before losses to Australia and hosts and eventual champions South Africa in a match best remembered for the brawl

COACH

KIERAN CROWLEY

Former All Black Kieran Crowley was a member of the New Zealand squad which won Rugby World Cup 1987. He was reserve full-back to John Gallagher and played the pool match against Argentina during a playing career in which he scored 105 points in 19 Tests. He coached New Zealand to victory at the 2007 Under 19 World Championship and was coach of the Taranaki province. He was appointed by Rugby Canada after Rugby World Cup 2007 and took up his position in April 2008, guiding the Canucks to the 2011 Tournament in his native New Zealand and now to the 2015 edition in England.

Canada
www.rugbycanada.ca

PLAYING STRIP Red shirts with black collar and black shoulders, white shorts, red socks

FORM SINCE RUGBY WORLD CUP 2011

Played:	21
Won:	10
Lost:	11
Drawn:	0
Winning percentage:	47.61%
Points for:	464
Points against:	430
Points scored per match:	22.10
Points conceded per match:	20.48
Biggest victory:	52-8 v Portugal in Lisbon on November 23, 2013
Heaviest defeat:	42-12 v Samoa in Colwyn Bay on November 9, 2012
World Rugby Ranking (at Jan 2015):	18

RUGBY WORLD CUP PERFORMANCES

1987	Pool stages
1991	Quarter-finals
1995	Pool stages
1999	Pool stages
2003	Pool stages
2007	Pool stages
2011	Pool stages

STAR PLAYER

DTH VAN DER MERWE

Position:	Centre or wing
Born:	April 28, 1986
	Worcester, South Africa
Club:	Glasgow Warriors (Sco)
Height:	1.83m (6ft)
Weight:	98kg (216lb)
Caps:	32
Points:	70 (14t)

If South Africa-born Daniel Tailliferrer Hauman van der Merwe can stay fit, Canada have a match-winner in their midst. His family emigrated to Canada in 2003 and he pledged his allegiance to his new country. A short stint at Saracens followed his impressive showing at Rugby World Cup 2007 but Van der Merwe has firmly established himself as a crowd favourite with Glasgow Warriors. He is the Scottish side's record try-scorer despite a succession of ankle and shoulder injuries limiting his game time. Van der Merwe is an elusive runner and strong tackler and is often used at outside centre by Canada to enable him to get on the ball as often as possible.

PLAYERS TO WATCH

1. TYLER ARDRON
Age: 24; *Position:* flanker/number 8 and captain; *Club:* Ospreys (Wal); *Caps:* 17; *Points:* 10 (2t)

2. JAMIE CUDMORE
Age: 36; *Position:* lock; *Club:* Clermont Auvergne (Fra); *Caps:* 33; *Points:* 10 (2t)

3. JAMES PRITCHARD
Age: 35; *Position:* full-back; *Club:* Bedford (Eng); *Caps:* 59; *Points:* 597 (18t 102c 101p)

4. TAYLOR PARIS
Age: 22; *Position:* wing; *Club:* Agen (Fra); *Caps:* 12; *Points:* 25 (5t)

5. ADAM KLEEBERGER
Age: 31; *Position:* flanker; *Club:* BC Bears (Can); *Caps:* 38; *Points:* 20 (4t)

which saw Rees and Snow sent off. A tournament-best 72-11 win over Namibia in Toulouse was not enough to advance from the pool stage at Rugby World Cup 1999 in France as it followed defeats to both France and Fiji. In 2003 in Australia, Canada were drawn with Wales, New Zealand, Italy and Tonga in their pool. The battle with the Azzurri was tight but Canada fell to a five-point defeat, and were unable to progress despite recovering with a victory over Tonga in their fourth and final contest of the Tournament.

Canada failed to sparkle at Rugby World Cup 2007, their first without Rees and Charron, losing three of their four matches to finish bottom of the pool. Japan came from behind in a 12-12 draw – the second in Rugby World Cup history and first for 20 years – which prevented the Canucks from recording a victory. It was the first time they had returned home from a Rugby World Cup without a single win and the disappointment prompted a coaching change, with Ric Suggitt replaced by former New Zealand Under-19 coach Kieran Crowley.

Canada's reputation was restored at Rugby World Cup 2011 when, with bearded flanker Adam Kleeberger to the fore, they opened with a 25-20 defeat of Tonga, who went on to beat eventual finalists France. Another draw with Japan was sandwiched between heavy defeats to Les Bleus and the All Blacks.

Since the last Tournament, Canada have gone close to beating established nations, most notably against Scotland in Toronto in June 2014, when a late Greig Laidlaw penalty secured victory for the visitors. France, Ireland, Italy and Romania are their opponents in Pool D and it is not beyond Canada to sneak through to the knockout stages for a second time.

Canada celebrate their victory over Tonga at Rugby World Cup 2011

Romania

Romania have a proud record as one of only 12 teams to have competed at every Rugby World Cup. They have so far been unable to make a dent on the world stage, with their best return to date being one win in the pool stages, and they face another tough task this time.

RUGBY ROMANIA

Romania
www.frr.ro

PLAYING STRIP Yellow shirts, blue shorts, blue socks

FORM SINCE RUGBY WORLD CUP 2011

Played:	32
Won:	22
Lost:	9
Drawn:	1
Winning percentage:	70.31%
Points for:	718
Points against:	480
Points scored per match:	22.44
Points conceded per match:	15.00
Biggest victory:	71-0 v Ukraine in Bucharest on March 31, 2012
Heaviest defeat:	34-3 v USA in Bucharest on November 24, 2012
World Rugby Ranking (at Jan 2015)	17

RUGBY WORLD CUP PERFORMANCES

1987	Pool stages
1991	Pool stages
1995	Pool stages
1999	Pool stages
2003	Pool stages
2007	Pool stages
2011	Pool stages

Rugby World Cup 2015 offers Romania the chance to show they are on the way back to the heady days of the 1980s, when they were a genuine force on the international Rugby stage.

The Romanian Revolution in 1989 changed the face of Rugby in the country completely, leaving the national side at rock bottom and needing to rebuild from the ground up. Before that time, the state funded top club sides CSA Steaua Bucuresti and Dinamo Bucharest, with the teams predominantly made up of players serving in the police and army. It made for a strong national side, which defeated Wales, Scotland and France in the run-up to the first Rugby World Cup in 1987. That Tournamant saw Romania open with a 21-20 victory over Zimbabwe, but they failed to maintain their momentum as they were brushed aside 55-12 by eventual finalists France before being knocked out after a 55-28 defeat by Scotland.

Following the Romanian Revolution and the overthrow of Nicolae Ceauşescu's communist regime in 1989, state funding fell away for the country's top two teams, while several of their leading players lost their lives during the conflict, including captain Florica Murariu. An army officer who won 69 caps for his country and starred at Rugby World Cup 1987 with two tries, he was shot dead at a roadblock aged 34 in December 1989.

Despite the upheaval, in 1990 Romania defeated France for the first time on French soil and went on to beat Fiji 17-15 at Rugby World Cup 1991. Again they could only claim one win though, suffering pool-stage defeats by France and Canada, while RWC 1995 offered them no solace whatsoever as they were beaten in all three of their pool matches by Canada, South Africa and Australia. It coincided with a decline of home-based players in what has sometimes been called a lost generation of Romanian Rugby.

Despite their struggles at the highest level, Romania won the inaugural European Nations Cup in 2000 but, by the following year, they were overhauled by Georgia in that competition before being defeated 134-0 by England at Twickenham in an autumn international.

In 2002, French coach Bernard Charreyre took the reins of the national side and reinvigorated them, leading the Oaks to European Nations Cup success and qualification for Rugby World Cup 2003. However, despite

COACH

LYNN HOWELLS

Welsh-born former Pontypridd player Lynn Howells is the man charged with changing Romania's fortunes at the Rugby World Cup. Howells was Wales' assistant coach under Graham Henry during Rugby World Cup 1999 and briefly took the reins in 2001 when Henry was coach of the British and Irish Lions. His time at international level was followed by spells in charge of Pontypridd, Cardiff, Celtic Warriors, Italian side Leonessa, Edinburgh and Doncaster. He was appointed as the new coach of Romania on January 14 2012 and secured an extended contract as a result of Romania's results in the European Nations Cup. Howells, who also coaches Bucharest Wolves, will relish his return to Wembley for the match against Ireland. It will be his first time back at the London venue since Wales denied England the Six Nations Grand Slam with a famous win in 1999.

STAR PLAYER

ION PAULICA

Position:	Prop
Born:	January 10, 1983, Braila, Romania
Club:	Perpignan (Fra)
Height:	1.83m (6ft 0in)
Weight:	119kg (262lb)
Caps:	68
Points:	5 (1t)

Ion Paulica started his career with Steaua Bucuresti before joining Bath in 2007. He spent two seasons at The Rec before switching to London Irish. Paulica was loaned to Championship club London Welsh for the 2012/13 season and in April 2013 it was announced he would be joining Top 14 side Perpignan. The 32-year-old is an experienced hand in Rugby World Cup competition, having played at the 2003, 2007 and 2011 editions, and fills the important role of tighthead as a seasoned campaigner with good knowledge of top-level Rugby in both France and England. This knowledge will be invaluable to his side against Les Bleus, Ireland and Italy.

as they failed to defend their title, but a narrow 25-24 victory over Italy — their first over a Six Nations side — gave them a boost, and they continued to sit comfortably in the top 20 of the World Rugby Rankings.

Qualification for Rugby World Cup 2007 in France came courtesy of finishing level on points with Georgia in the 2005/06 European Nations Cup but a bonus-point 24-18 loss to Italy was followed by a 42-0 defeat against Scotland before Romania claimed a narrow 14-10 win over Portugal. Their pool-stage exit was again confirmed, though, when they were brushed aside 85-8 by a ruthless New Zealand side.

The Oaks had to work hard to make sure of their qualification for Rugby World Cup 2011 in New Zealand but clinched their place by defeating Tunisia 56-13 in the repechage, before seeing off Uruguay 60-33 on aggregate. In the main Tournament, Romania were defeated 25-9 by Georgia, 67-3 by England, 43-8 by Argentina and 34-24 by Scotland to exit at the pool stage for the seventh consecutive time.

Avoiding an eighth early exit looks another tough ask at Rugby World Cup 2015 when Romania will line up against France, Ireland, Italy and Canada but securing two wins and automatic entry to Rugby World Cup 2019 looks a more realistic ambition.

an upturn in fortune, Romania were brushed aside in Australia and again won only one pool game, a 37-7 victory over Namibia after their exit from the competition had already been sealed. It came after losses against Ireland (45-17), Argentina (50-3) and Australia (90-8), with Romania earning

the unwanted title of leaking the fastest try in Rugby World Cup history when Elton Flatley scored after only 18 seconds. Charreyre paid for the results with his job.

Romania continued to struggle and were defeated by Portugal and Russia in the 2003/04 European Nations Cup

PLAYERS TO WATCH

1. HORATIU PUNGEA
Age: 29; *Position:* prop; *Club:* Scarlets (Wal); *Caps:* 21; *Points:* 0

2. MIHAI LAZAR
Age: 28; *Position:* prop; *Club:* Castres (Fra); *Caps:* 42; *Points:* 5 (1t)

3. MIHAI MACOVEI
Age: 28; *Position:* lock/flanker; *Club:* Baia Mare (Rom); *Caps:* 57; *Points:* 42 (8t, 1c)

4. IONUT DUMITRU
Age: 22; *Position:* wing; *Club:* Bucharest Wolves (Rom); *Caps:* 14; *Points:* 15 (3t)

5. CATALIN FERCU
Age: 28; *Position:* full-back; *Club:* Saracens (Eng); *Caps:* 75; *Points:* 140 (28t).

Romania were beaten in all four pool matches at Rugby World Cup 2011

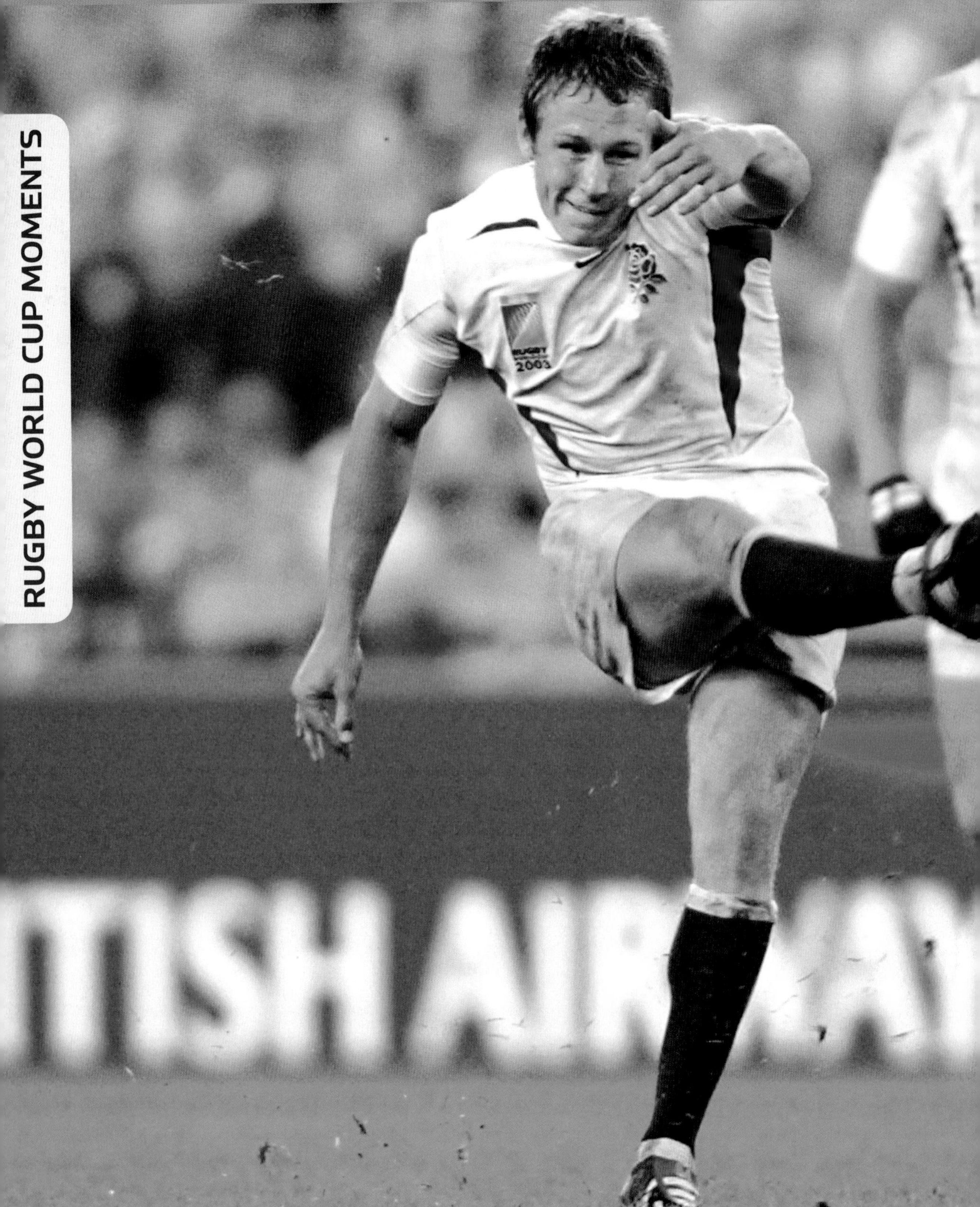
RUGBY
2003

WILKINSON ON TOP OF THE WORLD
NOVEMBER 22, 2003, TELSTRA STADIUM, SYDNEY

It was wholly appropriate that arguably English Rugby's most revered icon should create England's greatest moment as his drop goal 26 seconds from the end of extra-time saw Clive Woodward's class of 2003 crowned world champions. Fly-half Jonny Wilkinson rifled a right-footed strike between the posts on a Saturday night in Sydney to thwart hosts Australia 20-17 in a classic case of cometh the hour, cometh the man. The teams had been locked at 14-14 and then 17-17, yet England seized the moment as scrum-half Matt Dawson made a telling break before flanker Neil Back's pass set up a Martin Johnson charge. The ball came back via Dawson for ice-cool Wilkinson to land the kick that sent English Rugby fans into orbit.

Jonny Wilkinson lets fly with his 'weaker' right foot to score the all-important drop goal

Above: Wales wing George North became the youngest try-scorer in Rugby World Cup history in 2011

Left: South Africa legend Bryan Habana has more than 100 caps and 50 tries to his name

Right: Sergio Parisse has become one of the most respected forwards in the modern Game

Far right: National coach Steve Hansen believes All Blacks wing Julian Savea is even better than New Zealand icon Jonah Lomu

THE STARS TO WATCH

Throughout its 28-year existence, Rugby World Cup has provided a global platform for players to perform in the biggest matches when the stakes are at their highest. Superstars have been forged in the fires generated by ferocious intensity and staggering standards demanded by the greatest Rugby show on earth. Rugby World Cup heroes can be listed among the Game's most illustrious names – players such as Jonah Lomu, Jonny Wilkinson, John Eales, David Campese, Francois Pienaar and Richie McCaw – and England 2015 will be no exception. The following section highlights some of the candidates to join the list of Tournament greats.

Julian Savea New Zealand

The comparisons with Jonah Lomu are inevitable but regardlesss of how he matches up to his boyhood favourite, there is little doubt that Julian Savea is one of the most prolific try-scorers in international Rugby.

FACTS AND FIGURES

Born:	August 7, 1990, Wellington, New Zealand
Position:	Wing
Club:	Wellington (NZL)
Height:	1.92m (6ft 4in)
Weight:	108kg (238lb)
Caps:	33
Debut:	v Ireland at Eden Park, Auckland, on June 9, 2012
Points:	150 (30t)

Julian Savea first arrived on the All Blacks' radar as a teenager playing at the national Sevens final for Wellington College in 2006. The young winger played just two minutes in the tournament, thrown on as a substitute in the final, but his eye-catching display included a barnstorming run that had national Sevens coach Gordon Tietjens asking questions.

Two years later, Savea was selected for the New Zealand secondary schools team and joined the Hurricanes academy squad before enhancing his fast-growing reputation as he helped New Zealand Under-20s to the Junior World Championship title with eight tries in the tournament. His performances earned him the Junior Player of the Year Award and a place in the Wellington Lions squad for the 2010 ITM Cup.

Already being compared to New Zealand great Jonah Lomu, it was not long before Savea made his full Test debut for his country against Ireland in June 2012. Savea scored three tries at Eden Park that day – the first All Black to do so against Ireland – and since then he has established himself as undeniably the most feared finisher in world Rugby.

His astonishing record of 30 tries in 33 matches for New Zealand includes eight scores against both England and Argentina, four against Ireland and two against Australia. There is far more to Savea's armoury than just crossing the whitewash though, and while

he may not be the biggest winger around, he more than makes up for it in power, speed and agility. There are no obvious weaknesses to Savea's game – his awareness, catching, off-load and tackling make him a strong defender and excellent on the counter-attack.

The comparisons with Lomu continue to gather more weight with every try he scores. "I think he's probably better than Lomu," New Zealand head coach Steve Hansen said ahead of the team's Rugby Championship match against South Africa in October. "Jonah was a great player but I think Julian has got more to his game to be honest and that's saying something. I genuinely believe that. He's very good going back, under the high ball, with the ball on the ground, as well as being a great carrier so I think he's right up there."

Savea maintains the face of humility regarding the comparison, insisting his boyhood idol will always be the master of the All Black wing, but if he can match Lomu's Tournament record of eight tries which he set at Rugby World Cup 1999, defending champions New Zealand could again be unstoppable.

Julian Savea scored a hat-trick of tries on his Test debut and has not looked back since

Bryan Habana South Africa

Widely considered to be the fastest man in Rugby, South Africa wing Bryan Habana has been frightening opposition defences ever since he made his Test debut at Twickenham more than 10 years ago.

FACTS AND FIGURES

Born: .... June 12, 1983,
Johannesburg, South Africa
Position: .... Wing
Club: .... Toulon (Fra)
Height: 1.80m (5ft 11in)
Weight: 94kg (207lb)
Caps: 106
Debut: .... v England at Twickenham
on November 20, 2004
Points: 285 (57t)

Few players have made such an impact on their international debut as Bryan Habana did against England in November 2004. South Africa lost the match against the then-world champions but Habana, aged 21, came off the bench at Twickenham and scored with his first touch of the ball, racing past Josh Lewsey to touch down a consolation try. His performance earned him a starting spot against Scotland a week later and, after scoring twice at Murrayfield, Habana never looked back.

Formerly a scrum-half or centre, he now has more than a century of caps to his name, finding his feet on the wing where his electric pace and darting step make him a nightmare for any defender. He started all 12 Tests for his country in 2005 and scored 12 tries but it was at Rugby World Cup 2007 that Habana wrote his name into his country's history books. Equalling Jonah Lomu's Tournament record of eight tries, Habana fired South Africa to Rugby World Cup glory and his contribution was recognised with the World Rugby Player of the Year Award.

Habana can run the 100m in less than 11 seconds and his rapid reputation was put to the test when he was filmed for charity keeping pace with a cheetah and, in a separate video, outrunning a jumbo jet down the runway. Habana registered another milestone at Rugby World Cup 2011 when he passed Joost van der Westhuizen's long-standing record of 38 Test tries for South Africa and became the first Springbok to reach 50 when he scored twice against Samoa in June 2013.

"It is a wonderful effort, to score 50 tries in a career at all levels of Rugby is great, but to score 50 for your country in Tests is outstanding," said Springboks captain Jean de Villiers after the match. "He is a classy player, but has also put in a lot of hard work over the years. There always seems to be magic when he touches the ball." South Africa coach Heyneke Meyer added: "There is something about Bryan that when you put him in a Bok jersey, he's extraordinary."

The winger lifted the Top 14 and Heineken Cup trophies with Toulon in 2014 and has shown no sign of letting up. South Africa are up against Samoa, Scotland, Japan and the USA in Pool B and, if they qualify, could meet England, Australia or Wales in the quarter-finals. Habana has previously notched 19 tries against those three opponents and will be desperate to add a few more to his total in what may be his final Rugby World Cup.

Bryan Habana has passed the 50 mark as his country's all-time leading try-scorer

Israel Folau Australia

He has already featured at a Rugby League World Cup and now, having successfully switched codes after a stint in Australian Rules football, Israel Folau is set for the global stage again.

FACTS AND FIGURES

Born:	April 3, 1989, Minto, Australia
Position:	Full-back
Club:	Waratahs (Aus)
Height:	1.93m (6ft 4in)
Weight:	103kg (227lb)
Caps:	29
Debut:	v British and Irish Lions in Brisbane on June 22, 2013
Points:	85 (17t)

Israel Folau was hardly an unknown quantity when he switched from Rugby League to sign for Union side New South Wales Waratahs in 2013. He had been the youngest player ever to appear for Melbourne Storm when he made his debut aged 18 in 2007 and went on to smash the record for most tries in a debut season with 21. Those displays saw him handed the Rookie of the Year Award and also a place in the Australian Test side, where he scored two tries on debut in a record-breaking 58-0 defeat of New Zealand.

He appeared at the 2008 Rugby League World Cup before a move to Brisbane Broncos in 2009 and Folau's potency only increased as he scored 37 tries in 39 appearances for his new club. Speculation continued to mount regarding a potential code-switch but when Folau finally left Rugby League in 2010, it was to Australian Football League side Greater Western Sydney. After struggling to find his best form for the Giants, Folau finally announced his decision to move to Rugby Union and sign for the Waratahs.

A call-up to the Australian Test side soon followed and he scored two superb tries on his debut against the British and Irish Lions in June 2013. The first came with his second touch of the ball, brilliantly finishing off a counter-attack in the corner but the second was the pick of the pair as he stepped inside Jonathan Sexton before speeding past Alex Corbisiero and Leigh Halfpenny to touch down.

Australia lost but the game had heralded a breakthrough for a new star in 15-man Rugby.

After the match, Wallabies coach Robbie Deans said: "He has a lot of confidence to do the things that he does and he has a real physical stature so he's not intimidated. He's got fast feet, he's quick, he's got a great off-load, so when you've got that capacity to play that tends to slow the game down. It slows the defence down because they're conscious of all the options, and he is very good at taking the options. He is a talent – we need to get him into the game."

The full-back continued his scintillating form with a record-equalling 10 tries in his first year with the Wallabies and his tally has increased at a rapid rate. Folau's pace, acceleration, jump and strength make him a lethal weapon to the back-line. Cementing his place as one of the most powerful runners in world Rugby, Folau will be crucial to Australia's hopes of escaping a difficult pool and has never been one to shy away from a challenge.

Israel Folau made an immediate impact with two tries on his Test debut against the Lions

Owen Farrell **England**

Being the son of a famous Rugby father has not proved to be a burden for England fly-half Owen Farrell and he has long since been regarded as one of the brightest prospects in English Rugby.

FACTS AND FIGURES

Born: ....September 24, 1991,
Billinge, England
Position: ....Fly-half, centre
Club: ....Saracens (Eng)
Height: 1.88m (6ft 2in)
Weight: 96kg (211lb)
Caps: 29
Debut: ....v Scotland at Murrayfield
on February 4, 2012
Points: 290 (2t, 35c, 69p, 1dg)

Given his standing in English Rugby, it is hard to believe Owen Farrell is only 23 years of age. Son of England assistant coach Andy Farrell, the young fly-half has already earned 29 caps for England, made his debut for the British and Irish Lions, played in a Heineken Cup final and won a Premiership title.

Farrell became the then youngest player to play English professional Rugby when he made his senior Saracens debut in the 2008 Anglo-Welsh Cup aged 17, but it was not until three years later that injury problems thrust him into the club's first team. Despite his tender years, he made the No. 10 shirt his own, guiding Sarries to their first ever Premiership title and kicking 17 points in the final against Leicester. The breakthrough campaign also saw Farrell picked for England Under-20s who won the 2011 Six Nations Grand Slam and made the final of the Junior World Championship. It was no surprise when he was nominated for both the Premiership and Rugby Players' Association Young Player of the Year Awards that year.

England, still searching for a long-term successor to Jonny Wilkinson, were immediately alerted to Farrell's confident performances and in February 2012, Stuart Lancaster handed the 20-year-old his Test debut against Scotland. Often hailed for showing experience beyond his years, Farrell's pin-point kicking, tenacious tackling and intelligent positional sense are all attributes well-suited to the tactical demands of the international Game. His nerves of steel were there for all to see in England's historic 38-21 victory over New Zealand in 2012 as Farrell kicked four penalties, a conversion and a drop goal to end the All Blacks' 20-match unbeaten run.

Perhaps Farrell's most accomplished international display to date, though, came during last year's Six Nations when his commanding performance inspired a 29-18 win over Wales. Before that game, Lancaster made clear the esteem in which he holds his No. 10. "He has what very few young players have, particularly in the fly-half position, that big-game temperament and the ability to rise to the occasion," Lancaster said. "He doesn't seem fazed by an occasion. He has been outstanding in terms of providing leadership and direction to the team. He leads that defensive line and that defensive press very well."

Farrell's versatility has seen him used at inside centre at club level and it is a position he can play for England too given his awareness and ability to dictate territory with the boot. The home fans are expecting England to go far at Rugby World Cup 2015 and with a tough pool to navigate, they will be relying on Farrell to deliver.

Owen Farrell has become a central figure for England despite still being only 23

Johnny Sexton Ireland

A European champion and a key member of the Lions squad which triumphed in Australia in 2013, Johnny Sexton has become a mainstay of the Ireland team since featuring at Rugby World Cup four years ago.

FACTS AND FIGURES

Born: ....July 11, 1985,
Dublin, Ireland
Position: ....Fly-half
Club: ....Racing Métro (Fra)
Height: 1.88m (6ft 2in)
Weight: 92kg (202lb)
Caps: 47
Debut: .... v Fiji at Croke Park, Dublin
on November 21, 2009
Points: 423 (8t, 49c, 93p, 2dg)

Johnny Sexton made his Ireland debut against Fiji in November 2009 after catching the eye during three impressive years at Leinster. In 110 appearances for the province, Sexton scored 1,015 points and won three European Cups, two PRO12 titles and a Challenge Cup.

He burst onto the scene as an early substitute for Leinster in the 2009 Heineken Cup semi-final when he inspired his side to a 25-6 victory against fierce rivals Munster at Croke Park. Sexton then started the final against Leicester and more than justified his place, kicking a stunning drop goal from the half-way line and the winning penalty as Leinster won 19-16 and lifted their first European Cup.

The fly-half left his homeland for Racing Métro in 2013 but the French club failed to enjoy the same success and after much speculation, he announced his decision to return to Leinster when his contract expires at the end of the 2014/15 campaign. Ireland coach Joe Schmidt's control over how often his players turn out for their provinces means Sexton should arrive at Rugby World Cup 2015 fresh and raring to lead his side beyond the quarter-finals for the first time in eight attempts.

A superb passer off both hands, tenacious in the tackle and a world-class kicker, Sexton has become the heartbeat of the Ireland team in recent years. He initially had to share the No.10 jersey with Ireland stalwart Ronan O'Gara and was limited to two starts at Rugby World Cup 2011 but made the shirt his own in the 2012 Six Nations. He shone as Ireland won the 2014 Six Nations, scoring two tries and kicking a further seven points in a nail-biting 22-20 victory in France. Sexton was also the first-choice fly-half for the British and Irish Lions on their successful tour of Australia in 2013. He started all three Tests and scored a try in the decisive match in Sydney as the Lions won 2-1.

His partnership with scrum-half Conor Murray has underpinned Ireland's resurgence but equally important is Sexton's close relationship with Schmidt, whom he worked under for three seasons at Leinster. "This is going into our fifth season working together," Sexton said after Ireland beat South Africa 29-15 in November. "He's won a lot and we've won a lot, the four trophies with Leinster and one with Ireland, and six finals with Leinster. But it's not just the trophies. It really helps that the out-half and the coach have a good relationship."

Ireland have been drawn in Pool D with France, Italy, Canada and Romania and will need Sexton firing on all cylinders if they are finally to go beyond the last eight at a Rugby World Cup.

Johnny Sexton and coach Joe Schmidt have worked together at provincial and national level

George North Wales

Already in the Rugby World Cup record books for his exploits as a teenager in New Zealand, George North has continued to develop into one of the world's top performers during the past four years.

FACTS AND FIGURES

Born: ....April 13, 1992,
King's Lynn, England
Position: ....Wing
Club: ....Northampton (Eng)
Height: 1.93m (6ft 4in)
Weight: 109kg (240lb)
Caps: 45
Debut: ....v South Africa at Millennium
Stadium, Cardiff on November 13, 2010
Points: 95 (19t)

England's loss has most definitely been Wales' gain after George North moved from the country of his birth at the age of two and has gone on to establish himself as one of the most talented wingers in world Rugby. He progressed through the age groups in the Wales set-up and never considered pulling on any shirt other than a red one, before making his Wales debut in November 2010 aged just 18. He wasted no time in making a name for himself, scoring two tries and setting up another in a narrow defeat by South Africa.

North suffered a shoulder injury soon after but came back better than ever as he became the first teenager anywhere in the world to score 10 Test tries, including two against England at Twickenham in a warm-up match for Rugby World Cup 2011.

Wales defied the odds to reach the semi-finals in New Zealand and North continued to break records as he became the youngest try-scorer in the Tournament's history when he crossed the whitewash twice as a substitute against Namibia. "He's got a massive future, he's going to score a lot of tries," said Warren Gatland after the game and North has more than fulfilled the Wales coach's prophecy.

The powerhouse was an integral part of Wales' Grand Slam success in the 2012 Six Nations and again a year later when the side defended their title. His brilliant displays earned him a starting spot for the winning British and Irish Lions in Australia in 2013 and North justified his selection with arguably one of the best tries in Lions history as he collected a high kick before running 60 metres, dodging a handful of Wallabies on his way to the line. The winger added another score in the final Test and his personal battle with Israel Folau – at one stage he appeared to be running with the Wallaby full-back hoisted on his shoulders – was one of the highlights of the series.

Many will be looking forward to the battle recommencing in Pool A as Wales take on Australia, along with England, Fiji and Uruguay. North, who can also play at centre, brings a winning pedigree to the side having lifted both the Premiership title and the European Challenge Cup with Northampton in 2014. "George is an outstanding talent," said Northampton coach Jim Mallinder when the club signed North in April 2013. "Despite still being at the start of his career he has shown repeatedly that he has the ability and temperament to succeed at the highest level."

Wales wing George North became the youngest try-scorer in Rugby World Cup history in 2011

Thierry Dusautoir France

Born in the Ivory Coast to an Ivorian mother and French father, Thierry Dusautoir was a late starter in Rugby and nothing has been predictable about his journey to the very top of the sport.

FACTS AND FIGURES

Born: ....November 18, 1981,
Abidjan, Ivory Coast
Position: ....Flanker
Club: ....Toulouse (Fra)
Height: 1.88m (6ft 2in)
Weight: 99kg (218lb)
Caps: 70
Debut: ....v Romania in Bucharest
on June 17, 2006
Points: 30 (6t)

Thierry Dusautoir moved to France aged 10 and did not take up Rugby until he was 16, preferring to play other sports including judo. The flanker signed for CA Bordeaux-Bègles-Gironde in 2001 and US Colomiers in 2003 while studying for a degree in chemical engineering. In 2004, he finally decided to turn professional and joined Biarritz. He played in the Heineken Cup final in 2006 when Biarritz were edged out 23-19 by Munster but there was some consolation as the French outfit lifted the Top 14 title.

It was Toulouse, though, where Dusautoir played his Rugby the following season and where an international career would flourish. He was called into the France squad and marked his debut with a try in a 62-14 victory over Romania in June 2006.

A stand-out performance in a Rugby World Cup 2007 warm-up match against England was not enough to earn Dusautoir a start in the team's opening match of the Tournament against Argentina but a 17-12 defeat saw him swiftly elevated to the first XV for subsequent wins against Ireland and Namibia. France made it out of the pool and Dusautoir cemented his place in the side during a superb 20-18 victory over New Zealand in the last eight. Trailing by 10 points at half-time, Dusautoir initiated the second-half comeback with a try and statistics after the game showed he had made 38 of his team's 299 tackles – a new French record. France lost to England 14-9 in the semi-finals but Dusautoir had been the find of the Tournament.

His dynamism and energy has since been used on both sides of the back row and he stood in as captain during the 2009 summer tour of Australia and New Zealand and led the side to a famous 27-22 win against the All Blacks in Dunedin. Dusautoir was named permanent skipper in the autumn and starred as France registered another impressive 20-13 victory over South Africa in Toulouse. Les Bleus' momentum gathered pace in 2010 when they won the Six Nations Grand Slam, with captain Dusautoir starting every match.

He helped Toulouse to Top 14 glory in 2011 and Dusautoir produced the goods at his second Rugby World Cup later that year, including a try in the Final but France were edged out 8-7 by New Zealand. Dusautoir was subsequently named as the World Rugby Player of the Year.

Thierry Dusautoir led France to the 2011 Final and scored a try in their narrow defeat

Nicolás Sánchez **Argentina**

The leading points scorer in the 2014 Rugby Championship is the key source of creativity in the Argentina squad and dangerous with the boot, as Australia discovered to their cost last year.

FACTS AND FIGURES

Born: ....October 26, 1988,
San Miguel de Tucuman, Argentina
Position: ....Fly-half
Club: .... Toulon (Fra)
Height: 1.77m (5ft 10in)
Weight: 83kg (183lb)
Caps: 30
Debut: ....v Uruguay in Santiago
on May 21, 2010
Points: 230 (2t, 26c, 48p, 8dg)

Since making his Argentina debut in May 2010, Nicolás Sánchez has grown into Los Pumas' most accomplished and reliable performer. After playing for the Pampas XV in the Vodacom Cup, Sánchez moved to Top 14 side Bordeaux-Bègles in 2011, where he scored more than 100 points before announcing his decision to sign for European champions Toulon in 2014.

Sánchez is only 1.77 metres tall but his tenacious, combative style of play embodies the Argentine ethos and he was the top tackler in the 2013 Rugby Championship. The fly-half is also a creative force, eager to direct play with his excellent kicking and pin-point passes and he was the highest points scorer in the Rugby Championship last year. As Argentina have tried to adopt a more expansive, attacking style of play, Sánchez has thrived on the extra freedom he has been given.

His defensive capabilities will be tested to the full against New Zealand in Pool C but in matches against Tonga, Georgia and Namibia, Sánchez should be able to show the attacking qualities for which he is so renowned. He at least has some Rugby World Cup experience to call on, having been part of the squad which travelled to New Zealand four years ago but were eliminated by the hosts at the quarter-final stage. Sánchez enjoyed only five minutes of action, coming on as a late replacement during the 43-8 victory over Romania in Invercargill, but is guaranteed to be a mainstay of the team this time around if he remains fully fit.

Sánchez has played 14 Rugby Championship matches, scoring 87 points including nine conversions and 23 penalties. "We have a feeling we are gaining more and more respect with each passing game," Sánchez said after South Africa were pushed all the way. His prediction was backed up in October when Argentina's confidence heading towards Rugby World Cup 2015 was boosted by their first ever victory in the Rugby Championship as Australia were defeated 21-17. Sánchez starred, kicking three penalties and one crucial conversion from close to the touchline as the team ended an eight-match losing streak with their first win over the Wallabies since 1997. On a personal level, Sánchez finished as the top-scorer in the tournament to highlight his growing credentials as one of the leading players in the Game.

Los Pumas should qualify for the knockout stages at Rugby World Cup 2015 but to go beyond the quarter-finals for only the second time in their history, Sánchez will need to be at his creative best and hope those around him can reach similar levels of performance.

Nicolás Sánchez was top scorer in last season's Rugby Championship

Stuart Hogg *Scotland*

Scotland may have struggled in recent years but the same cannot be said of Stuart Hogg, who has become an increasingly important member of the team since being handed his senior international debut in 2012.

FACTS AND FIGURES

Born: ....June 24, 1992, Melrose, Scotland
Position: ....Full-back
Club: ....Glasgow Warriors (Sco)
Height: 1.80m (5ft 11in)
Weight: 93kg (205lb)
Caps: 27
Debut: ....v Wales at Millennium Stadium, Cardiff on February 12, 2012
Points: 43 (8t, 1p)

Stuart Hogg has been Scotland's stand-out performer during a difficult couple of years for the national team. He follows a number of Scottish internationals to have learned his trade at Hawick where he first started playing Rugby as a junior before representing Scotland at Under-17, Under-18 and Under-20 levels. After joining the Glasgow Warriors Elite Development Squad, Hogg was handed his professional debut aged 18 in February 2011 and earned selection for the Junior World Championship in Italy that summer.

Hogg's breakthrough campaign came in 2011/12 when he was regularly selected in the PRO12 and also enjoyed a taste of elite competition in the Heineken Cup. His confident displays saw him called up to the Scotland training squad ahead of the 2011 Six Nations but it was not until February 2012 that Hogg made his full Test debut, on the wing in a 27-13 defeat to Wales at the Millennium Stadium in Cardiff.

Two weeks later, in his next international match and this time at full-back, Hogg became Scotland's youngest try-scorer in 79 years when he crossed the line against France.

He has also played at fly-half and centre in his career but it is at No.15 that he has made a name for himself. Perhaps his most memorable score to date came at Twickenham against England in February 2013 when he sprinted half the length of the field before collecting his own kick and touching down.

A distant relative of legendary Manchester United footballer George Best, he comes from a talented family, with father John and brother Graham having both played Rugby at a high level. Hogg was one of four Scotland players to be called up for the successful British and Irish Lions tour to Australia in 2013, when he was the youngest player in the squad. He did not feature in the three Tests but he did produce a man-of-the-match performance against the Combined County XV, when he scored a try from fly-half.

His creativity, defence and excellent reading of the game will be crucial to Scotland's hopes of qualifying from Pool B, where they have been drawn alongside South Africa, Samoa, Japan and the USA.

They will need to be at their best to make the knockout stages but the team are rejuvenated under Vern Cotter. "We have different structures in place and we are trying to play a different brand of Rugby," Hogg explained in November. "Get quick ball, play on the front foot, put the carrot in front of the donkey by kicking the ball in behind them and keeping the forwards going forward. It is an exciting way to play."

Stuart Hogg was the youngest man in the 2013 British and Irish Lions squad

Sergio Parisse Italy

Few players on duty at Rugby World Cup 2015 can boast as much experience of the Tournament as Sergio Parisse, with the Italy captain now preparing for his fourth edition of the event.

FACTS AND FIGURES

Born: ....September 12, 1983,
La Plata, Argentina
Position: ....Number 8
Club: ....Stade Français (Fra)
Height: 1.96m (6ft 5in)
Weight: 110kg (242lb)
Caps: 108
Debut: ....v New Zealand in Hamilton
on June 8, 2002
Points: 63 (12t, 1dg)

Sergio Parisse has been among the world's best loose forwards for a generation. The Azzurri's captain and talisman, he became the first Italy player to be short-listed for World Rugby's Player of the Year Award in 2008 and has been a beacon of world-class quality for his country for the best part of 10 years. Parisse's father Sergio was also an accomplished player, winning an Italian Championship title with L'Aquila in 1967 before his job took him to Argentina, where Sergio Jnr was born.

It was Italy, though, where Parisse felt at home and he made his name during four years at Treviso, where his impressive performances earned him his first Italy cap aged 18 in June 2002 in a 64-10 defeat to New Zealand. The number 8 played at Rugby World Cup 2003 and it was there he scored his first Test try against Canada, although Italy failed to make it out of the pool stage.

A move to Stade Français followed in 2005, joining team-mates Mauro and Mirco Bergamasco, but Parisse continued to deliver his most inspired performances in international colours.

In 2008, he earned his 50th Italy cap against England in the Six Nations aged 24 and was also named captain by coach Nick Mallett, taking over from Marco Bortolami. Italy beat Scotland 23-20 in Rome but finished bottom of the table under Parisse's leadership – a fate they were unable to avoid again in 2009. A serious knee injury ruled him out of most of the 2009/10 Top

14 season and the 2010 Six Nations but Parisse returned for the 2011 tournament and was as influential as ever as Italy recorded a thrilling 22-21 victory over France before a year later managing to deflect the wooden spoon to Scotland after a 13-6 victory in the final round of matches.

A year later, Parisse was banned from the tournament's third round onwards after receiving a 40-day suspension for insulting a referee during a match for Stade Français but the Italy skipper was still able to make a telling contribution, scoring a try in a stunning 23-18 opening win over France. A second success against Ireland saw them finish fourth in 2013 but a disappointing campaign in 2014 meant the Azzurri returned to the foot of the table. Parisse featured in his third consecutive Rugby World Cup in 2011 and scored two tries as Italy finished third in the pool after victories against the USA and Russia. Defeats to Australia and Ireland, however, ensured the team missed out on a place in the knockout phase.

A powerful ball-carrier, brilliant out of hand and nimble on his feet, Parisse is a player who has stood out for his country under pressure and in times of adversity. Now he would like nothing more than to lead his country into the last eight for the first time.

Still only 31, Sergio Parisse will be playing in his fourth Rugby World Cup

Jacques Burger Namibia

Not even a two-year long injury struggle has diminished Jacques Burger's love for the game and the fearless flanker, famed for his tackling power, is again ready to put his body on the line for Namibia.

FACTS AND FIGURES

Born: .... July 29, 1983, Windhoek, Namibia
Position: .... Back row
Club: .... Saracens (Eng)
Height: 1.88m (6ft 2in)
Weight: 106kg (234lb)
Caps: 30
Debut: .... v Zambia in Nchingola on August 14, 2004
Points: 25 (5t)

Jacques Burger's Rugby career has been something of a rollercoaster ride but it is his fitness rather than form that has been up and down. The flanker aggravated a knee problem while playing for Saracens in February 2011, sparking a two-year injury battle that had the player doubting whether he would ever play again. It is testament to Burger's passion that he played through the pain barrier at Rugby World Cup 2011 and proof of his talent that he was still named in the Tournament's top five players, having made 64 tackles in four matches.

The back-rower was Saracens' Player of the Year in the club's Premiership-winning campaign in 2010/11 but it was not until the start of the 2013/14 season that Burger was finally declared fully fit again. His superb performances helped Saracens finish top of the table and he broke a Premiership record when he made an astonishing 37 tackles against Exeter Chiefs in September 2013. He was an instrumental presence in Saracens' run to the Heineken Cup final, delivering a superb performance in a 46-6 victory over Clermont Auvergne at Twickenham in the semi-final.

"Jacques' story is incredible," said Saracens boss Mark McCall after the game. "He was out of Rugby for 18 months and this time last year when he came back he didn't look right, it looked like it may be over for him. People don't know what he does every day, because he ices his knee about five times a day and it's an incredible sacrifice for him to play in games like this. He was an inspiration – you know he'll give everything he has for the team."

Burger is best known for his thundering collisions and rampaging runs forward but he is also a technical player, capable of playing anywhere across the back row. He made his Namibia debut against Zambia in August 2004 and has gone on to play 30 matches for his country, scoring five tries along the way.

"It's incredible to represent your country at a Rugby World Cup, it's something I decided to do and it's something you always remember when you finish Rugby," he said about risking his fitness to play in 2011. "It's really important to me, I love Namibia, I love playing for my country. I don't get paid playing for my country, I do it because I'm a Namibian and because I want to play for my country whenever I get the chance."

It is that passion that will see Burger feature at the third Rugby World Cup of his career.

Jacques Burger has defied injury to play for Namibia for more than 10 years

Jamie Cudmore Canada

Playing at a fourth Rugby World Cup will be a special achievement for Jamie Cudmore and another step on a remarkable journey for the veteran, who has used Rugby to transform his life.

FACTS AND FIGURES

Born: ....September 6, 1978,
Squamish, Canada
Position: ....Lock
Club: ....Clermont Auvergne (Fra)
Height: 1.96m (6ft 5in)
Weight: 116kg (256lb)
Caps: 33
Debut: ....v USA in Chicago
on July 13, 2002
Points: 10 (2t)

Jamie Cudmore will have to be at his bludgeoning best if Canada are to avoid a sixth consecutive exit in the pool stages. The veteran lock has long been his country's most influential player but the road to stardom has not always been so smooth.

Growing up in Squamish in British Columbia, Cudmore was the bill collector for a local drug dealer and then served a year in a juvenile detention centre after being found guilty of assault. Taking up Rugby with a local fourth division social side to stay in favour with his boss, Cudmore took a liking to the oval ball and headed south to Vancouver where he began to turn his life around.

"In a sense, yes, Rugby saved me," Cudmore told the official Rugby World Cup 2015 website. "It gave me an outlet for my rambunctiousness. Rugby got me on the right track and I'm certainly glad it did."

The son of English parents, Cudmore will be looking to steal some of the limelight in his family during Rugby World Cup 2015, with one of his brothers, Daniel, having starred in the *X-Men* and *Twilight* films. If the Canadian colossus is fit and on form, he will pose a threat to any side. The Clermont Auvergne player received his first cap for Canada in a qualifying match for Rugby World Cup 2003 against the USA and the 36-year-old, who has previously lined up for Llanelli and FC Grenoble, scored his first try for the men's national team in 2004.

His remarkable journey took him and Clermont to a Heineken Cup final in 2013 but the trophy belonged to Toulon after a nail-biting 16-15 defeat in Dublin.

Ironically nicknamed 'Cuddles' in the dressing room, Cudmore is renowned for his aggression, strength and blistering power in the ruck. While he has left his troubled past behind, the 6ft 5in lock retains a ruthless streak that has earned him a reputation as one of the world's toughest operators. Cudmore's ferociousness can sometimes spill over — he was handed two suspensions in the 2010/11 season including a 70-day ban for stamping on Jacques Burger. He has played in three consecutive Rugby World Cups, having featured in the 2003, 2007 and 2011 Tournaments, but is yet to experience the competition's knockout phase. Canada have not made it past the pool stage since 1991 when they scored six tries to beat Tonga 37-4 before losing 29-13 to New Zealand in the quarter-finals, and they face a tough challenge once again but with Cudmore leading the charge, anything is possible.

Jamie Cudmore has come from a troubled background to star

FIJI STUN WALES IN THRILLER
SEPTEMBER 29, 2007, STADE DE LA BEAUJOIRE, NANTES

Wales were expected to secure a Rugby World Cup quarter-final date with South Africa but Fiji won a thriller in the Nantes sunshine to call time on Gareth Jenkins' coaching reign. Fiji's big hits and strong running led to tries from Akapusi Qera, Vilimoni Delasau and Kele Leawere as Wales' open style played into the hands of the Pacific Islanders. Scores from Alix Popham, Shane Williams, Gareth Thomas – who became the first man to win 100 caps for his country – and Mark Jones brought Wales back into it before Martyn Williams' 73rd-minute interception try looked the clincher. Graham Dewes powered over from close range for the game's ninth try, though, to settle it 38-34 in Fiji's favour and heap further south sea island embarrassment on Wales, who had lost to the Samoans in the 1991 and 1999 Tournaments.

Wales forward Gethin Jenkins (1) and Michael Owen (19) look on as Fiji celebrate

Above: Despair for France and delight for New Zealand after the final whistle in the Rugby World Cup 2011 Final in Auckland

Left: South Africa captain John Smit and coach Jake White celebrate with the Webb Ellis Cup in 2007

Right: Match-winner Jonny Wilkinson and team-mate Will Greenwood jump for joy at the end of the 2003 Final

HISTORY LESSON

Rugby World Cup has become the fulcrum of the Game since it was launched in 1987, contested every four years and showcasing the very best teams and finest players. There have been seven Tournaments, four different world champions and one major winner – the Game itself. Rugby World Cup history is alive with memorable matches, individual genius, record-breaking exploits, raw emotion, high drama and supporters' stories to last a lifetime.

Rugby World Cup 1987 New Zealand and Australia

The inaugural Rugby World Cup in New Zealand and Australia saw seven of the 16 places filled by IRFB members – the two hosts, England, Scotland, Ireland, Wales and France – and nine other countries invited. South Africa were kept away by their international sports boycott, and New Zealand triumphed over France in the Final.

The pressure was on New Zealand and Australia to shine at the first Rugby World Cup after they had been awarded joint status to stage the Tournament.

The first match was between New Zealand and Italy at Eden Park in Auckland and the All Blacks' large 70-6 victory was illuminated by wing John Kiwan beating virtually the entire Azzurri defence on a 70-metre run to the line.

The All Blacks were untested in Pool 3, which also brought wins over Fiji (74-13) and Argentina (46-15), but Australia had to work harder in Pool 1, where they opened up with a 19-6 victory over England at the Concord Oval in Sydney. David Campese and Simon Poidevin scored tries and the boot of Michael Lynagh did the rest, with Mike Harrison managing a try for England.

Both sides saw off Japan and the United States in their other pool matches but England had to settle for a quarter-final against Wales.

The Welsh won all their Pool 2 games, with Mark Ring's try proving the difference in a hard-fought 13-6 victory over Ireland in windy Wellington, before Tonga (29-16) and Canada (40-9) were also seen off.

Ireland claimed second spot in the pool by scoring six tries to beat Canada 46-19 while Brendan Mullin raced in for a hat-trick in the 32-9 defeat of Tonga.

As the pattern of one-sided matches continued – half of the 24 matches across the four pools saw one team score 40 points or more – France and Scotland racked up the points against Romania and Zimbabwe to progress from Pool 4. Their meeting in Christchurch produced the first Rugby World Cup draw, France bettering Scotland by three tries to two in a 20-20 draw and winning the pool by virtue of a better points difference.

Scotland's second spot sent them to Christchurch where they would meet rampant hosts New Zealand

RUGBY WORLD CUP HEROES

GRANT FOX (NEW ZEALAND)

The All Blacks were a formidable outfit at the inaugural Rugby World Cup, possessing both fearsome forwards and powerful runners in the back division. But they also had a metronomic goal-kicker who barely wasted a single shot at goal. Grant Fox kicked 126 points in New Zealand's six matches – setting a Tournament record which still stands seven editions later – and went on to amass a career total of 645 points from 46 Tests for the All Blacks. Fox's ability to keep the scoreboard ticking over meant that no-one was able to get close to New Zealand in that first Tournament.

Serge Blanco scores his famous last-gasp try in France's semi-final win in Sydney

TOURNAMENT STATISTICS

Host nations:......Australia and New Zealand
Dates:.....................May 22–June 20, 1987
Teams:...16
Matches:..32
Overall attendance:.........................448,318
(14,010 per match)

Pool 1

Team	W	D	L	F	A	Pts
Australia	3	0	0	108	41	6
England	2	0	1	100	32	4
United States	1	0	2	39	99	2
Japan	0	0	3	48	123	0

Pool 2

Team	W	D	L	F	A	Pts
Wales	3	0	0	82	31	6
Ireland	2	0	1	84	41	4
Canada	1	0	2	65	90	2
Tonga	0	0	3	29	98	0

Pool 3

Team	W	D	L	F	A	Pts
New Zealand	3	0	0	190	34	6
Fiji	1	0	2	56	101	2
Italy	1	0	2	40	110	2
Argentina	1	0	2	49	90	2

Pool 4

Team	W	D	L	F	A	Pts
France	2	1	0	145	44	5
Scotland	2	1	0	135	69	5
Romania	1	0	2	61	130	2
Zimbabwe	0	0	3	53	151	0

Quarter-finals

New Zealand	30-3	Scotland
Australia	33-15	Ireland
France	31-16	Fiji
Wales	16-3	England

Semi-finals

France	30-24	Australia
New Zealand	49-6	Wales

Bronze Final

Wales	22-21	Australia

THE FINAL

New Zealand 29-9 France

Tries: Jones, Kirk	Try: Berbizier
Kirwan	
Con: Fox	Con: Camberabero
Pens: Fox (4)	Pen: Camberabero
Drop: Fox	

LEADING POINTS SCORERS

1	126	Grant Fox (NZL)
2	82	Michael Lynagh (Aus)
3	62	Gavin Hastings (Sco)
4	53	Didier Camberabero (Fra)
5	43	Jonathan Webb (Eng)

LEADING TRY SCORERS

1=	6	Craig Green (NZL)
=	6	John Kirwan (NZL)
3=	5	Matt Burke (Aus)
=	5	Mike Harrison (Eng)
=	5	John Gallagher (NZL)
=	5	Alan Whetton (NZL)
=	5	David Kirk (NZL)

with their goal-kicker Grant Fox at his supreme best. Fox landed six penalties and converted the tries of Alan Whetton and John Gallagher in a 30-3 stroll.

France also eased through with four tries to beat Fiji 31-16 and Australia ran in another four tries to knock out Ireland 33-15. The tightest of the quarter-finals was at Brisbane's Ballymore ground but Wales emerged 16-3 winners with Gareth Roberts, Robert Jones and John Devereux – who was fast becoming known for his meaty hand-offs – claiming tries against an England side who simply ran out of ideas.

Wales were no match for New Zealand in their Brisbane semi-final as the All Blacks ran in eight tries, with Kirwan and Wayne Shelford scoring half of them in a 49-6 romp. Insult was added to Welsh injury when second row Huw Richards became the first player to be sent off at a Rugby World Cup for swinging a punch at Gary Whetton.

The other semi-final in Sydney was

an epic affair as Australia led three times but on each occasion they were foiled by French flair. Les Bleus ran in four tries and a late moment of magic from French full-back Serge Blanco, who crossed in the corner, clinched a shock 30-24 victory.

Wales needed a late Adrian Hadley try and Paul Thorburn's touchline conversion to beat Australia 22-21 and claim third place, even though Wallaby flanker David Codey had been sent off in the early stages of the match in Rotorua.

All eyes were then on the Eden

Park Final and New Zealand carried the weight of expectation to run out 29-9 winners against France before a sell-out crowd of 48,000. Captain David Kirk, Michael Jones and Kirwan scored tries with the faultless Fox adding 17 points, the issue well and truly settled before Pierre Berbizier's late response. No-one could complain about the outcome as New Zealand had scored 298 points in six matches, 126 of them from Fox, and 43 tries while conceding only four on their way to becoming the first winners of the Webb Ellis Cup.

Rugby World Cup 1991 England

The Rugby World Cup came to the northern hemisphere for the first time as the desire to share in the occasion saw five nations – England, Ireland, Scotland, Wales and France – stage matches. The Tournament again involved 16 teams but this time eight came through qualifying – and some were to leave their mark on established nations.

The inaugural Rugby World Cup in 1987 had seen many one-sided matches as the IRFB members piled up the points and cut a swathe through the Tournament but, four years on, the bigger Rugby nations would not have it all their own way.

England and reigning champions New Zealand opened the Tournament in a heavyweight collision at Twickenham – fearsome flanker Michael Jones scoring the only try in an 18-12 victory for the All Blacks – but it was events in Cardiff three days later which sparked the competition into life.

Wales had finished third at Rugby World Cup 1987 in New Zealand and were expected to ease past Western Samoa at their Cardiff Arms Park citadel in Pool C but the debut-making Samoans ran out 16-13 winners on one of the darkest days in Welsh Rugby history. Western Samoa also pushed Australia close in a 9-3 defeat and their 35-12 victory over Argentina booked them a quarter-final spot. Wales tried to save themselves against the Wallabies but it was more humiliation than redemption as a David Campese-inspired Australia ran in six tries to romp home 38-3 and eliminate the co-hosts.

Western Samoa's heroics were repeated by Canada, who surprised Fiji with a 13-3 victory in Bayonne on their way to a last-eight appearance. Inspired by the boot of fly-half Gareth Rees, Canada kept the theme of the emerging nations going and beat Romania 19-11 before running France close in a 19-13 loss.

Scotland and Ireland had few problems progressing from Pool B where they had Japan and Zimbabwe for company. Their winning margins were reminiscent of some of the scores from four years earlier with the only debate being who would win the section and avoid Australia in the quarter-final, Scotland booking top spot with a 24-15 victory.

New Zealand's opening-day win over England had put them in charge

RUGBY WORLD CUP HEROES

DAVID CAMPESE (AUSTRALIA)

David Campese was not everyone's cup of tea as he was as outspoken off the pitch as he was dangerous with ball in hand on it, but there was no disputing his brilliance. The Wallabies winger lit up the 1991 Tournament with six tries, including two in the quarter-final victory against Ireland and one in the semi-final which helped down arch-rivals and holders New Zealand. Even from his station out on the wing he could decide games and former Ireland fly-half Tony Ward described him as "the Maradona and Pele of Rugby rolled into one". He was duly named Player of the Tournament for Rugby World Cup 1991.

Australia celebrate and England despair at the final whistle at Twickenham

TOURNAMENT STATISTICS

Host nations:............England, France, Ireland,
                       Scotland and Wales
Dates:................October 3-November 2, 1991
Teams: ....16 (33 qualifying)
Matches:...32
Overall attendance:...................1,060,065
                       (average 33,127 per match)

Pool A

Team	W	D	L	F	A	Pts
New Zealand	3	0	0	95	39	9
England	2	0	1	85	33	7
Italy	1	0	2	57	76	5
United States	0	0	3	24	113	3

Pool B

Team	W	D	L	F	A	Pts
Scotland	3	0	0	122	36	9
Ireland	2	0	1	102	51	7
Japan	1	0	2	77	87	5
Zimbabwe	0	0	3	31	158	3

Pool C

Team	W	D	L	F	A	Pts
Australia	3	0	0	79	25	9
W Samoa	2	0	1	54	34	7
Wales	1	0	2	32	61	5
Argentina	0	0	3	38	83	3

Pool D

Team	W	D	L	F	A	Pts
France	3	0	0	82	25	9
Canada	2	0	1	45	33	7
Romania	1	0	2	31	64	5
Fiji	0	0	3	27	63	3

Quarter-finals

England	19-10	France
Scotland	28-6	Western Samoa
Australia	19-18	Ireland
New Zealand	29-13	Canada

Semi-finals

England	9-6	Scotland
Australia	16-6	New Zealand

Bronze Final

New Zealand	13-6	Scotland

THE FINAL

Australia	12-6	England
Try: Daly		Pens: Webb (2)
Con: Lynagh		
Pens: Lynagh (2)		

LEADING POINTS SCORERS

1	68	Ralph Keyes (Ire)
2	66	Michael Lynagh (Aus)
3	61	Gavin Hastings (Sco)
4	56	Jonathan Webb (Eng)
5	44	Grant Fox (NZL)

LEADING TRY SCORERS

1=	6	David Campese (Aus)
=	6	Jean-Baptiste Lafond (Fra)
3=	4	Tim Horan (Aus)
=	4	Brian Robinson (Ire)
=	4	Iwan Tukalo (Sco)
=	4	Rory Underwood (Eng)

of Pool A, although they were given a fright before beating Italy 31-21 in Leicester.

England saw off Italy (36-6) and the United States (37-9) to set up a quarter-final date with France in Paris. France were on a revenge mission after being denied in a Grand Slam decider at Twickenham seven months earlier but Mickey Skinner's extraordinary tackle on Marc Cécillon, with the scores tied at 10-10 and France pressing, took the wind out of home sails and England went on to win 19-10.

The last-eight stage was where the Rugby World Cup fairytale would end for Canada and Western Samoa. Canada's reward for their progress was a quarter-final meeting with New Zealand but they went down 29-13 and Western Samoa were not the force they had been earlier as they were beaten 28-6 by Scotland. Australia completed the semi-final line-up after beating Ireland in Dublin in one of the greatest matches ever

witnessed in the Tournament. Two tries from Campese gave Australia a 15-12 lead in a hard-fought encounter but with five minutes left on the clock Ireland flanker Gordon Hamilton charged 40 yards down the touchline to score. Hamilton was mobbed by team-mates and supporters alike and Ralph Keyes converted from the touchline, but Michael Lynagh took advantage of a quickly-taken tap penalty to squeeze in at the corner for a breathless 19-18 victory.

The two semi-finals were derby affairs with Scotland meeting England at an emotion-charged Murrayfield and Australia tackling New Zealand at

Lansdowne Road. Rob Andrew's drop goal sealed a 9-6 victory for England with Scotland's Gavin Hastings left to rue a close-range penalty miss, while Australia administered the All Blacks' first-ever Rugby World Cup defeat as Campese and Tim Horan crossed in a 16-6 win.

New Zealand overcame Scotland 13-6 in Cardiff to take third place and the Twickenham Final was also a low-scoring affair with Australia prop Tony Daly scoring the solitary try in the Wallabies' 12-6 victory over an England side who veered away from their power game and tried to run the ball more.

Rugby World Cup 1995 South Africa

The first Rugby World Cup to be held in one country was also the first to feature South Africa after their international sports exile was ended and the hosts were carried to the Final on a wave of emotion. They then beat New Zealand 15-12 after extra-time before Francois Pienaar famously received the Webb Ellis Cup from Nelson Mandela.

South Africa marked their Rugby World Cup bow with a 27-18 victory over Australia in Cape Town and confidence in the Host Nation began to grow as they had few problems negotiating Pool A, which also brought wins over Romania (21-8) and Canada (20-0).

Australia duly took second spot in the pool to book a quarter-final berth and they were joined by England and Western Samoa, the latter emulating their 1991 last-eight appearance by overcoming Italy (42-18) and Argentina (32-26). Rob Andrew's 24-point haul – six penalties and two

drop goals – gave England a 24-18 victory over Argentina, who scored two tries, and Italy were then beaten 27-20 before Rory Underwood scored twice in a 44-22 victory over Western Samoa.

Pool C proved to be the most eventful section where Jonah Lomu revealed his awesome running power with two tries in a 43-19 victory over Ireland. Lomu was rested for the next game against Japan which saw New Zealand run in a record 21 tries – winger Marc Ellis also setting a Rugby World Cup individual best with six tries – to win 145-17. It remains

the most points scored by any one side at the Tournament. The All Blacks also saw off Wales 34-9 and the Welsh fell at the pool stage for the second consecutive time when they succumbed 24-23 to Ireland in Johannesburg.

France and Scotland made it out of Pool D, a pool also including Tonga and the Ivory Coast. Les Bleus beat Scotland 22-19 in the group finale in Pretoria to take top place but the section was best remembered for being tainted by tragedy. Ivory Coast winger Max Brito was paralysed after sustaining a neck injury against Tonga

RUGBY WORLD CUP HEROES

FRANCOIS PIENAAR (SOUTH AFRICA)

There was no doubting that New Zealand phenomenon Jonah Lomu was the star of the show in 1995, the giant winger scoring seven tries with four of them coming in the semi-final against England when the opposition's captain Will Carling labelled him "a freak". But South Africa captain Francois Pienaar proved the Tournament's ultimate hero as the flanker helped his side to Rugby World Cup glory with his brilliant individual displays and then received the Webb Ellis Cup after the tense Final from the country's President Nelson Mandela, who was wearing the famous Springboks green and gold jersey bearing the No.6 worn by the triumphant skipper.

England full-back Mike Catt's futile attempt to halt Jonah Lomu's charge to the line

TOURNAMENT STATISTICS

Host nation: ....South Africa
Dates: ....May 25-June 24, 1995
Teams: ....16 (52 qualifying)
Matches: 32
Overall attendance: 936,990
(average 29,281 per match)

Pool A

Team	W	D	L	F	A	Pts
South Africa	3	0	0	68	26	9
Australia	2	0	1	87	41	7
Canada	1	0	2	45	50	5
Romania	0	0	3	14	97	3

Pool B

Team	W	D	L	F	A	Pts
England	3	0	0	95	60	9
W Samoa	2	0	1	96	88	7
Italy	1	0	2	69	94	5
Argentina	0	0	3	69	87	3

Pool C

Team	W	D	L	F	A	Pts
New Zealand	3	0	0	222	45	9
Ireland	2	0	1	93	94	7
Wales	1	0	2	89	68	5
Japan	0	0	3	55	252	3

Pool D

Team	W	D	L	F	A	Pts
France	3	0	0	114	47	9
Scotland	2	0	1	149	27	7
Tonga	1	0	2	44	90	5
Ivory Coast	0	0	3	29	172	3

Quarter-finals

France	36-12	Ireland
South Africa	42-14	Western Samoa
England	25-22	Australia
New Zealand	48-30	Scotland

Semi-finals

South Africa	19-15	France
New Zealand	45-29	England

Bronze Final

France	19-9	England

THE FINAL

South Africa	15-12	New Zealand (aet)
Pens: Stransky (3)		Pens: Mehrtens (3)
Drops: Stransky (2)		Drops: Mehrtens

LEADING POINTS SCORERS

1	112	Thierry Lacroix (Fra)
2	104	Gavin Hastings (Sco)
3	84	Andrew Mehrtens (NZL)
4	79	Rob Andrew (Eng)
5	61	Joel Stransky (RSA)

LEADING TRY SCORERS

1=	7	Marc Ellis (NZL)
=	7	Jonah Lomu (NZL)
3=	5	Gavin Hastings (Sco)
=	5	Rory Underwood (Eng)
5=	4	Thierry Lacroix (Fra)
=	4	Adriaan Richter (RSA)
=	4	Chester Williams (RSA)

and the unfortunate episode sparked a debate over whether Rugby nations like the west African country were developed enough to be competing at the Rugby World Cup.

The four quarter-finals produced a glut of points, starting with the clash between Ireland and France in Durban. Philippe Saint-André and Emile Ntamack scored tries and Thierry Lacroix kicked a record eight penalties in France's 36-12 win, while South Africa wing Chester Williams crossed four times as the Springboks overpowered Western Samoa 42-14.

New Zealand beat Scotland 48-30 in a game of nine tries – six for the All Blacks, three for Scotland – and the closest meeting saw England win a tension-filled affair against Australia, Andrew landing a 45-metre drop goal with the final kick of the match to triumph 25-22.

South Africa met France in the first of the semi-finals, where torrential rain had turned the King's Park pitch in Durban into a lake, Ruben Kruger's

solitary try proving the difference in a 19-15 victory.

New Zealand overcame England 45-29 in the other semi-final in Cape Town as Lomu resembled the class bully against players who were physically no match for him. The 20-year-old bulldozed his way past Tony Underwood, Will Carling and Mike Catt for one memorable try and scored another three as a global Rugby star was well and truly born.

France beat England 19-9 to take third place but all the attention was on Ellis Park in Johannesburg with South Africa, who had adopted the slogan 'one team, one nation' seeking to

reunite a nation bearing the scars of 40 years of apartheid.

In truth, the Final was a disappointing contest, kick cancelling out kick until Joel Stransky's extra-time drop goal sent the whole of South Africa into celebration.

The enduring image of the day came when President Nelson Mandela, clad in a Springbok jersey which for so long was the symbol of the 'white man's game', and who had spent 26 years as a political prisoner on Robben Island and in other prisons, presented the Webb Ellis Cup to captain Francois Pienaar as a nation was united by sport.

Rugby World Cup 1999 Wales

Wales and the new Millennium Stadium hosted the first Rugby World Cup staged during the Game's professional era. Several matches were also played in England, Scotland, Ireland and France as the Tournament was expanded to 20 teams, and there was no doubting Australia's dominance as they were crowned champions for a second time.

Rugby World Cup was bigger than ever in 1999 as the Tournament was expanded from 16 to 20 teams, in five pools of four. The five pool winners would progress, while five pool runners-up and the best third-placed team contested three play-off matches to complete the quarter-final picture.

A further new venture was a qualifying Repechage, whereby two places at the finals would be filled by teams from several that had finished runners-up in their respective qualifying regions. Tonga and Uruguay were the beneficiaries.

It was Wales that started the Tournament, defeating Argentina 23-18 at the £126millon, 75,000-capacity Millennium Stadium, and it did not take

long for the competition heavyweights to make a mark during pool stages that ultimately saw Australia, South Africa, New Zealand and France enjoy 100 per cent records, while Wales also progressed despite being beaten in Cardiff by Samoa for the second time in three Rugby World Cup Tournaments.

There were some historic achievements in the pool matches as 40-year-old Uruguay captain Diego Ormaechea marked his country's debut against Spain by scoring their first try, while Canada captain Gareth Rees featured in a fourth successive Rugby World Cup and Ireland hooker Keith Wood's four tries against the USA equalled the Rugby World Cup record for a forward in one game.

With the five pool winners confirmed, it meant that England – coached by Clive Woodward at his first Rugby World Cup – Scotland and Ireland all ventured into play-off territory and additional midweek fixtures, and two of them progressed. Jonny Wilkinson inspired England's 45-24 victory over Fiji, and Scotland beat Samoa 35-20, but Argentina were edged out Ireland 28-24 in Lens. It meant the Irish failed to reach the quarter-finals for the first time.

Wales' hopes of booking a first semi-final appearance since the inaugural Rugby World Cup disappeared against Australia in Cardiff, when Wallabies scrum-half George Gregan's try double underpinned a 24-9 success, and there was a remarkable scoring feat

RUGBY WORLD CUP HEROES

TIM HORAN (AUSTRALIA)

Tim Horan was Australia's centre of attention, a brilliant runner, distributor and game manager who hit peak form at Rugby World Cup 1999. Having made his Wallabies debut 10 years earlier, the Queenslander had grown into arguably the world's finest centre, and his performances made him Player of the Tournament in 1999. He had to overcome a horrendous knee injury during the mid-1990s that sidelined him for more than a year, and his standards at Rugby World Cup 1999 were exemplary, despite suffering food poisoning a night before Australia's semi-final win over South Africa. It was his second Rugby World Cup triumph.

Australia's 6ft 7in captain John Eales towers over the Queen at the presentation

TOURNAMENT STATISTICS

Host nation: .... Wales
Dates: .... October 1-November 6, 1999
Teams: .... 20 (65 qualifying)
Matches: 41

Pool A

Team	W	D	L	F	A	Pts
South Africa	3	0	0	132	35	9 *
Scotland	2	0	1	120	58	7 +
Uruguay	1	0	2	42	97	5
Spain	0	0	3	18	122	3

Pool B

Team	W	D	L	F	A	Pts
New Zealand	3	0	0	176	28	9 *
England	2	0	1	184	47	7 +
Tonga	1	0	2	47	171	5
Italy	0	0	3	35	196	3

Pool C

Team	W	D	L	F	A	Pts
France	3	0	0	108	52	9 *
Fiji	2	0	1	124	68	7 +
Canada	1	0	2	114	82	5
Namibia	0	0	3	42	186	3

Pool D

Team	W	D	L	F	A	Pts
Wales	2	0	1	118	71	7 *
Samoa	2	0	1	97	72	7 +
Argentina	2	0	1	83	51	7 +
Japan	0	0	3	36	140	3

Pool E

Team	W	D	L	F	A	Pts
Australia	3	0	0	135	31	9 *
Ireland	2	0	1	100	45	7 +
Romania	1	0	2	50	126	5
United States	0	0	3	52	135	3

* qualified for quarter-finals
+ qualified for quarter-final play-offs

Overall attendance: 1,556,572
(average 37,965 per match)

Quarter-final play-offs

England	45-24	Fiji
Scotland	35-20	Samoa
Argentina	28-24	Ireland

Quarter-finals

Australia	24-9	Wales
South Africa	44-21	England
New Zealand	30-18	Scotland
France	47-26	Argentina

Semi-finals

Australia	27-21	South Africa	(aet)
France	43-31	New Zealand	

Bronze Final

South Africa	22-18	New Zealand

THE FINAL

Australia	35-12	France

Tries: Tune, Finegan   Pens: Lamaison (4)
Cons: Burke (2)
Pens: Burke (7)

LEADING POINTS SCORERS

1	102	Gonzalo Quesada (Arg)
2	101	Matt Burke (Aus)
3	97	Jannie de Beer (RSA)
4	79	Andrew Mehrtens (NZL)
5	69	Jonny Wilkinson (Eng)

LEADING TRY SCORERS

1	8	Jonah Lomu (NZL)
2	6	Jeff Wilson (NZL)
3=	4	Keith Wood (Ire)
=	4	Philippe Bernat-Salles (Fra)
=	4	Viliame Satala (Fij)
=	4	Dan Luger (Eng)

achieved at the Stade de France when England took on South Africa. England headed to Paris for a second game in quick succession after defeating play-off opponents Fiji, with Woodward opting to start with Northampton's Paul Grayson at fly-half rather than Wilkinson, but it was Grayson's opposite number, Jannie de Beer, who took centre-stage through an astounding display of kicking accuracy. De Beer booted five drop goals in a 44-21 victory for the Springboks, smashing the previous Rugby World Cup record for one match, and he finished with 34 points.

The remaining two quarter-finals followed anticipated form as Christophe Lamaison scored 22 of France's points in a 47-26 defeat of Argentina – Xavier Garbajosa and Philippe Bernat-Salles each scored two tries – while New Zealand were predictably too strong for Scotland, winning 30-18 at Murrayfield.

The semi-finals provided two unforgettable encounters of contrasting styles, with both proving epic contests. Australia and South Africa contested the first semi-final at Twickenham, where de Beer and

Wallabies kicker Matt Burke rose to the occasion as two brilliantly-organised and committed teams fought each other to a standstill, including during a period of extra-time after it finished 21-21 at 80 minutes. De Beer kicked six penalties and a drop goal, while Burke landed eight penalties and fly-half Stephen Larkham dropped a goal to book Australia's place in the Final. The second semi-final at Twickenham 24 hours later appeared to be following

form as try-hungry powerhouse All Blacks wing Jonah Lomu helped drive his team into a solid lead, but France conjured a miracle, scoring 33 unanswered points at a rate of more than a point per minute to sink New Zealand 43-31.

France, though, had little left in the tank for the Final as Burke amassed another 25 points and Australia captain John Eales received the Webb Ellis Cup from Her Majesty the Queen.

Rugby World Cup 2003 Australia

England arrived at Rugby World Cup 2003 in Australia as favourites and, inspired by points machine Jonny Wilkinson, they duly delivered by beating the Wallabies after extra-time in a dramatic final in Sydney. England became the northern hemisphere's first world champions, while coach Clive Woodward was subsequently knighted.

Australia had staged a hugely successful 2000 Sydney Olympics, and once again the Australian public underpinned a memorable sporting event, with more than 1.8 million fans watching Rugby World Cup pool matches in 10 host cities from Perth to Townsville and Adelaide to Brisbane. The whole country appeared to immerse itself in what was a spectacular Tournament and one that produced a momentous climax when Jonny Wilkinson's drop goal seconds from the end of extra-time saw England beat Australia 20-17 in the Final.

England were drawn in the same pool as South Africa, and they knew victory over the Springboks in Perth would be critical in terms of their overall Tournament aspirations. Centre

Will Greenwood's try helped that result to materialise, while England also defeated Uruguay (111-13), Georgia (84-6) and Samoa (35-22). The Samoa match ended with England being summoned to attend a disciplinary hearing for briefly having 16 players on the pitch, but they avoided any points deduction.

Australia started their campaign in Pool A by defeating Argentina 24-8, and they went through the pool unbeaten, courtesy of subsequent wins against Romania, Namibia (142-0 – a Rugby World Cup record winning margin) in Adelaide when the Wallabies scored 22 tries, including five for full-back Chris Latham, and Ireland (17-16). The Irish also progressed to the last eight after edging past Argentina 16-15.

As expected, France proved the dominant force in Pool B, averaging 40 points a game in brushing aside rivals Scotland, Fiji, the United States and Japan. Scotland went through as runners-up, but Les Bleus' supremacy was graphically underlined by a 51-9 defeat of the Scots in Sydney.

New Zealand found themselves in Pool C, and there was added intrigue with chief pool rivals Wales being coached by New Zealander Steve Hansen. Their meeting in Sydney proved to be a Rugby World Cup epic as they delivered 90 points and 12 tries, trading touchdown for touchdown in exhilarating fashion before the All Blacks prevailed 53-37. New Zealand encountered far less trouble in their other games, seeing off Italy (70-7), Canada (68-6) and

RUGBY WORLD CUP HEROES

JONNY WILKINSON (ENGLAND)
Cometh the hour, cometh the man applied to Jonny Wilkinson before, during and after Rugby World Cup 2003. Arguably the biggest superstar northern hemisphere Rugby has ever seen, he arrived at the Tournament as England's proven and ultra-reliable match-winner, and even under the most severe of pressure he still delivered. Coach Clive Woodward knew and England knew that a fit and firing Wilkinson could apply the spectacular finishing touches to a well-oiled Rugby machine, and so it proved.

England captain Martin Johnson holds aloft the Webb Ellis Cup after a gripping Final

TOURNAMENT STATISTICS

Host nation:..Australia
Dates:...........October 10-November 22, 2003
Teams:.................................20 (80 qualifying)
Matches:...48

Overall attendance:..............................1,837,547
(average 38,282 per match)

Pool A

Team	W	D	L	F	A	Pts
Australia	4	0	0	273	32	18
Ireland	3	0	1	141	56	15
Argentina	2	0	2	140	57	11
Romania	1	0	3	65	192	5
Namibia	0	0	4	28	310	0

Pool B

Team	W	D	L	F	A	Pts
France	4	0	0	204	70	20
Scotland	3	0	1	102	97	14
Fiji	2	0	2	98	114	10
United States	1	0	3	86	125	6
Japan	0	0	4	79	163	0

Pool C

Team	W	D	L	F	A	Pts
England	4	0	0	255	47	19
South Africa	3	0	1	184	60	15
Samoa	2	0	2	138	117	10
Uruguay	1	0	3	56	255	4
Georgia	0	0	4	46	200	0

Pool D

Team	W	D	L	F	A	Pts
New Zealand	4	0	0	282	57	20
Wales	3	0	1	132	98	14
Italy	2	0	2	77	123	8
Canada	1	0	3	54	135	5
Tonga	0	0	4	46	178	1

Quarter-finals

New Zealand	29-9	South Africa
Australia	33-16	Scotland
France	43-21	Ireland
England	28-17	Wales

Semi-finals

Australia	22-10	New Zealand
England	24-7	France

Bronze Final

New Zealand	40-13	France

THE FINAL

England	20-17	Australia	(aet)

Try: Robinson — Try: Tuqiri
Pens: Wilkinson (4) — Pens: Flatley (4)
DG: Wilkinson

LEADING POINTS SCORERS

1	113	Jonny Wilkinson (Eng)
2	103	Frédéric Michalak (Fra)
3	100	Elton Flatley (Aus)
4	75	Leon MacDonald (NZL)
5	71	Chris Paterson (Sco)

LEADING TRY SCORERS

1=	7	Doug Howlett (NZL)
=	7	Mils Muliaina (NZL)
3	6	Joe Rokocoko (NZL)
4=	5	Will Greenwood (Eng)
=	5	Chris Latham (Aus)
=	5	Josh Lewsey (Eng)
=	5	Mat Rogers (Aus)
=	5	Lote Tuqiri (Aus)

Tonga (91-7), while Wales won three matches to secure a quarter-final place for the second successive Rugby World Cup.

The quarter-final shake-up meant Wales faced an encounter against their fierce and traditional rivals England at Brisbane's Suncorp Stadium and, although the form guide ultimately held true, Wilkinson and company were given a major fright as tries by Colin Charvis and Stephen Jones took Wales into a half-time lead before another key Greenwood try underpinned an English revival and an eventual 28-17 victory. The heavyweight last-eight clash paired New Zealand and South Africa together, yet it proved to be a one-sided affair as the All Blacks powered home 29-9. Leon MacDonald scored 16 points, including a try, and there were also touchdowns for wing Joe Rokocoko and hooker Keven Mealamu as a disappointing Springboks side headed for home. Elsewhere, Elton Flatley's 18 points helped Australia see off Scotland

33-16, while France overcame Ireland 43-21, with Freddie Michalak scoring 23 points.

If Australia were to keep alive hopes of becoming the first team in Rugby World Cup history to successfully defend the Webb Ellis Cup, they would have to do it the hard way as New Zealand blocked their path to the Final, but the Wallabies delivered an inspired display to triumph 22-10. A day later, England squeezed France into submission. As the rain fell in Sydney, so Wilkinson rammed home their supremacy with five penalties and three drop goals to

sink Les Bleus 24-7. It meant that one of sport's greatest rivalries — Australia versus England — was set for another full-blown airing in the Final, and it did not disappoint.

Australia led early through a Lote Tuqiri try, only for England to hit back when Jason Robinson touched down. Both teams had subsequent chances to prevail in normal time, but a battle of the boot between Wilkinson and Flatley meant the score was locked at 17-17 before Wilkinson landed the most famous drop goal in Rugby history and the Wallabies had no time to recover.

Rugby World Cup 2007 France

France won the bid to stage Rugby World Cup 2007, with four matches taking place in Cardiff and two in Edinburgh. There were shocks galore and the hosts never recovered from an opening loss to Argentina, while England staged a remarkable recovery to reach a second successive Final but could not deny South Africa a second world title.

Hosts France faced a huge weight of expectation when they took to the field against Argentina for the opening match of Rugby World Cup 2007 and it proved too much for them as Los Pumas secured a stunning 17-12 triumph that immediately put a proverbial cat among the pigeons. Argentina, with players like Agustín Pichot, Felipe Contepomi and Ignacio Corleto in their ranks, made a statement on day one, and they were to become unquestionably the Tournament's most-improved team.

If Los Pumas ruffled a few feathers, it was nothing compared

to what England managed. They arrived at the Tournament as defending champions following a dramatic extra-time triumph against Australia in the RWC 2003 Final in Sydney. Coaching supremo Sir Clive Woodward had departed, with Lancastrian Brian Ashton put in charge following an ineffective Andy Robinson reign.

England made a dismal start, struggling past the USA in Lens, then being on the receiving end of a 36-0 Springbok defeat, but somehow they recovered, defeating quarter-final opponents Australia in Marseille

before ending French interest at the semi-final stage.

While South Africa and England fought out the Final – it proved a try-less affair decided on penalties – New Zealand could only lick their wounds after making a dramatic, and for them, premature exit.

Graham Henry's squad had arrived in France as red-hot favourites, but Les Bleus sent them packing at the quarter-final stage in Cardiff after tries by Thierry Dusautoir and Yannick Jauzion secured a 20-18 victory. It was the first time in Rugby World Cup history that the All Blacks had bowed

RUGBY WORLD CUP HEROES

AGUSTÍN PICHOT (ARGENTINA)
Diminutive Los Pumas scrum-half Agustín Pichot was the embodiment of Argentine Rugby, a world-class player who led from the front on and off the pitch. A wonderful talent, he drove Argentina to achieving their finest Rugby World Cup performance in 2007. They defeated France twice, toppled Ireland and only bowed out at the semi-final stage against eventual winners South Africa. Wherever he played, whether for English club Bristol or the French pair Stade Français and Racing Métro, Pichot proved to be a consistently-brilliant performer on the pitch and a wonderful Rugby ambassador off it, with the 2007 Tournament the crowning glory of his outstanding career.

South Africa captain John Smit kisses the Webb Ellis Cup after the win over England

TOURNAMENT STATISTICS

Host nation: ....France
Dates: ....September 7-October 20, 2007
Teams: ....20 (91 qualifying)
Matches: 48

Overall attendance: 2,245,731
(average 46,786 per match)

Pool A

Team	W	D	L	F	A	Pts
South Africa	4	0	0	189	47	19
England	3	0	1	108	88	14
Tonga	2	0	2	89	96	9
Samoa	1	0	3	69	143	5
United States	0	0	4	61	142	1

Pool B

Team	W	D	L	F	A	Pts
Australia	4	0	0	215	41	20
Fiji	3	0	1	114	136	15
Wales	2	0	2	168	105	12
Japan	0	1	3	64	210	3
Canada	0	1	3	51	120	2

Pool C

Team	W	D	L	F	A	Pts
New Zealand	4	0	0	309	35	20
Scotland	3	0	1	116	66	14
Italy	2	0	2	85	117	9
Romania	1	0	3	40	161	5
Portugal	0	0	4	38	209	1

Pool D

Team	W	D	L	F	A	Pts
Argentina	4	0	0	143	33	18
France	3	0	1	188	37	15
Ireland	2	0	2	64	82	9
Georgia	1	0	3	50	111	5
Namibia	0	0	4	30	212	0

Quarter-finals

England	12-10	Australia
France	20-18	New Zealand
South Africa	37-20	Fiji
Argentina	19-13	Scotland

Semi-finals

England	14-9	France
South Africa	37-13	Argentina

Bronze Final

Argentina	34-10	France

THE FINAL

South Africa 15-6 England
Pens: Steyn   Pens: Wilkinson (2)
Montgomery (4)

LEADING POINTS SCORERS

1	105	Percy Montgomery (RSA)
2	91	Felipe Contepomi (Arg)
3	67	Jonny Wilkinson (Eng)
4	50	Nick Evans (NZL)
5	47	Jean-Baptiste Elissalde (Fra)

LEADING TRY SCORERS

1	8	Bryan Habana (RSA)
2	7	Drew Mitchell (Aus)
3=	6	Doug Howlett (NZL)
=	6	Shane Williams (Wal)
5=	5	Joe Rokocoko (NZL)
=	5	Vincent Clerc (Fra)
=	5	Chris Latham (Aus)

out before the semi-finals and they were joined on the long journey home by Australia, whose pack were given a torrid scrummaging time by England at Stade Velodrome, where Jonny Wilkinson's goal-kicking prevailed.

It meant that only South Africa were left to fly the Tri-Nations flag, being joined in the last four by England, France and Argentina, with New Zealand and Australia among a number of countries left to reflect on what might have been.

Ireland never got going in their pool, where losses to France and Argentina meant an early exit, while Wales also bowed out early after they were out-run by Fiji in Nantes. It proved a costly defeat not only for the squad, as coach Gareth Jenkins lost his job within 24 hours of that result following a meeting of senior Welsh Rugby Union officials, but Scotland did reach the quarter-finals following what was effectively an eliminator against Italy in St Etienne.

The Tournament also witnessed a number of battling displays by teams such as Tonga, who beat Samoa and ran both South Africa and England close, a wonderfully-committed Georgia side edged out only 14-10 by Ireland, and some memorable attacking moments provided by Portugal, who had qualified for the first time.

But while the Springboks, and their galaxy of talented players like Bryan Habana, Percy Montgomery and Victor Matfield under John Smit's inspired captaincy, deservedly reclaimed the Webb Ellis Cup they had won 12 years previously, it was Argentina – they beat France again

in the Bronze Final to finish third – who deserved every plaudit that went their way, especially skipper Pichot and coach Marcelo Loffreda.

The Final itself saw South Africa prevail through four Montgomery penalties and a long-range Francois Steyn strike, although England went desperately close to a try when wing Mark Cueto was ruled to have put a foot in touch as he crossed the line under pressure from a Danie Rossouw tackle, and it was ultimately Springboks skipper John Smit who lifted Rugby's golden prize high into the Paris night sky.

Rugby World Cup 2011 New Zealand

New Zealand had neither hosted nor won a Rugby World Cup since the inaugural Tournament in 1987 so when the country was awarded the 2011 edition, expectation was high that, after 24 years of hurt, the All Blacks would end a nation's suffering. They did just that, by the narrowest of margins, beating France 8-7 in a tense Final.

The collective mood in New Zealand in the weeks prior to Rugby World Cup 2011 was that of an excited child at Christmas. The earthquake that struck Christchurch in February of that year, killing 185 people, had tested the resolve of the nation and Rugby World Cup offered its people the chance to put the disaster behind them.

The All Blacks produced a thorough performance against Tonga in the Tournament opener to win 41-10. The match will be remembered for Israel Dagg announcing his arrival on the world stage by scoring two tries and making the New Zealand full-back jersey his own at the expense of Mils Muliaina. With the first pool match out of the way, the All Blacks stoked the nation's excitement further by beating Japan (83-7) and France (37-17) to guarantee their quarter-final place. On the eve of their final pool match against Canada, star fly-half Dan Carter suffered a Tournament-ending groin injury and, with one cruel snap of a tendon, it seemed as though the All Blacks' Rugby World Cup curse had struck again. With Colin Slade stepping into the No. 10 jersey, the All Blacks nevertheless crushed Canada 79-15 to top their pool.

France, meanwhile, slumped to a surprise 19-14 defeat to Tonga and only qualified for the quarter-finals after picking up more bonus points than their Pacific Island conquerors.

England topped Pool B by winning their pool matches against Argentina (13-9), Scotland (16-12), Georgia (41-10) and Romania (67-3), while Los Pumas won their encounter against Scotland (13-12) to also move into the last eight.

Pool C pitted Ireland and Australia against one another and the men in green eked out a 15-6 victory against Robbie Deans' side and topped the pool after also beating Italy (36-6), USA (22-10) and Russia (62-12).

In Pool D, South Africa and Wales vied for top spot and their crunch showdown went South Africa's way, the Springboks winning 17-16, while both teams secured victories over Fiji, Namibia and Samoa.

RUGBY WORLD CUP HEROES

RICHIE McCAW (NEW ZEALAND)

After guiding New Zealand to a disappointing Rugby World Cup 2007 quarter-final exit, Richie McCaw had something to prove when it was New Zealand's turn to stage the Tournament in 2011. McCaw was nursed through the pool matches, winning his 100th Test cap against France but aggravating a foot injury in the process. McCaw returned for the quarter-final victory over Argentina, before schooling David Pocock in the semi-final triumph over Australia. The combative flanker, one of the greats of New Zealand rugby history, then guided the All Blacks to final glory against France.

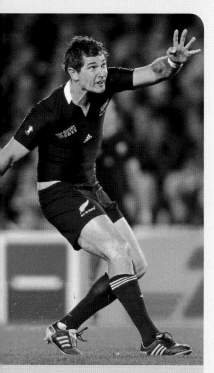

Fourth-choice fly-half Stephen Donald kicks a vital penalty in the Rugby World Cup 2011 Final

TOURNAMENT STATISTICS

Host nation: New Zealand
Dates: September 9-October 23, 2011
Teams: 20 (91 qualifying)
Matches: 48

Overall attendance: 1,477,294
(average 30,777 per match)

Pool A

Team	W	D	L	F	A	Pts
New Zealand	4	0	0	240	49	20
France	2	0	2	124	96	11
Tonga	2	0	2	80	98	9
Canada	1	1	2	82	168	6
Japan	0	1	3	69	184	2

Pool B

Team	W	D	L	F	A	Pts
England	4	0	0	137	34	18
Argentina	3	0	1	90	40	14
Scotland	2	0	2	73	59	11
Georgia	1	0	3	48	90	4
Romania	0	0	4	44	169	0

Pool C

Team	W	D	L	F	A	Pts
Ireland	4	0	0	135	34	17
Australia	3	0	1	173	48	15
Italy	2	0	2	92	95	10
USA	1	0	3	38	122	4
Russia	0	0	4	57	196	1

Pool D

Team	W	D	L	F	A	Pts
South Africa	4	0	0	166	24	18
Wales	3	0	1	180	34	15
Samoa	2	0	2	91	49	10
Fiji	1	0	3	59	167	5
Namibia	0	0	4	44	266	0

Quarter-finals

Wales	22-10	Ireland
France	19-12	England
Australia	11-9	South Africa
New Zealand	33-10	Argentina

Semi-finals

France	9-8	Wales
New Zealand	20-6	Australia

Bronze Final

Australia	21-18	Wales

THE FINAL

New Zealand	8-7	France
Try: Woodcock		Try: Dusautoir
Pen: Donald		Con: Trinh-Duc

LEADING POINTS SCORERS

1	62	Morné Steyne (RSA)
2	52	James O'Connor (Aus)
3	45	Kurt Morath (Tng)
4	44	Ronan O'Gara (Ire)
5	41	Piri Weepu (NZL)

LEADING TRY SCORERS

1 =	6	Chris Ashton (Eng)
=	6	Vincent Clerc (Fra)
3 =	5	Adam Ashley-Cooper (Aus)
=	5	Keith Earls (Ire)
=	5	Israel Dagg (NZL)
6 =	4	Mark Cueto (Eng)
=	4	Vereniki Goneva (Fij)
=	4	Richard Kahui (NZL)

Carter's Tournament-ending injury meant that, despite the All Blacks setting up a quarter-final against Argentina, the mood in New Zealand was nervous as questions over Slade's ability to cut it in international Rugby gripped the country. The nation need not have bothered with the conjecture, though, as Slade himself fell victim to a groin injury against Argentina and was also ruled out of the rest of the Tournament. Up stepped scrum-half Piri Weepu to kick seven penalties as New Zealand won 33-10.

Australia set up a semi-final encounter with the All Blacks by beating South Africa 11-9, France ended England's Tournament with a 19-12 victory to face Wales, who strolled to a 22-10 victory over Ireland.

New Zealand, now fielding third-choice fly-half Aaron Cruden, then produced the performance of the Tournament to beat Australia 20-6 and reach the Final, while Welsh captain Sam Warburton's dismissal in the first 20 minutes ultimately helped France edge to a 9-8 victory over Wales in the other semi-final.

The New Zealand media went into overdrive in the week-long wait until the Final as, despite France's spluttering performances, the fact that Les Bleus had stunned New Zealand in Rugby World Cups past was not lost on the public.

Come the day of the Final, Kiwi nerves were eased when Tony Woodcock touched down from a well-worked lineout move after 15 minutes. Then it was Cruden's turn to limp off with a knee injury so it was Stephen Donald, New Zealand's fourth-choice No. 10, who slotted home a penalty early in the second half to extend the All Blacks' lead to 8-0. France hit back immediately, with captain Thierry Dusautoir scoring a 47th-minute try that Francois Trinh-Duc duly converted to narrow New Zealand's lead to one point.

France were in the ascendancy and Trinh-Duc narrowly missed a penalty in the closing stages but the All Blacks ran down the clock and the 24-year wait for a second Rugby World Cup title was over.

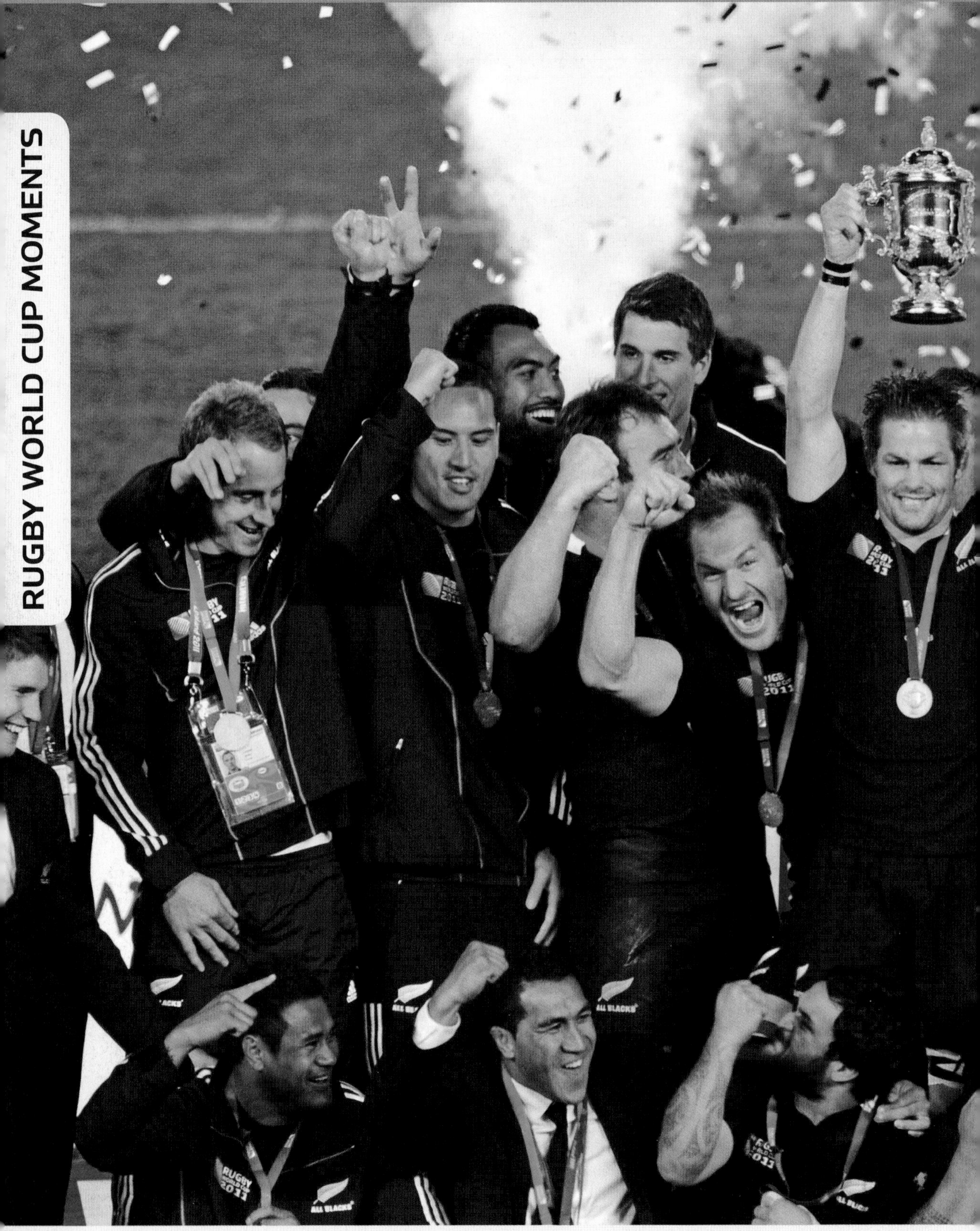
ALL BLACKS

ALL BLACKS TRIUMPH AGAIN
OCTOBER 23, 2011, EDEN PARK, AUCKLAND
··

New Zealand finally ended 24 years of Rugby World Cup hurt by beating France in the Eden Park Final – just as they had done in 1987. It was not pretty but Tony Woodcock's early try and a penalty from fourth-choice fly-half Stephen Donald were enough to see the All Blacks home against opponents who had just scraped past 14-man Wales in the semi-final. France produced their best performance of the Tournament after captain Thierry Dusautoir's try with half an hour left set up a nerve-tingling finale. Francois Trinh-Duc missed a long-range penalty before desperate defence saw the All Blacks hang on for Richie McCaw to lift the Trophy and spark jubilant scenes all over New Zealand.

The All Blacks celebrate as Richie McCaw lifts the Webb Ellis Cup

Above: All Blacks powerhouse Jonah Lomu has scored more tries in Rugby World Cup history than any other player with 15, and shares the record for most in a single Tournament with Bryan Habana. They scored eight each in 1999 and 2007 respectively

Left: England prop Jason Leonard's 22 appearances is a Rugby World Cup record – but he never scored a try

Top right: The famous Adelaide Oval cricket scoreboard shows the final score after the biggest victory in Rugby World Cup matches, Australia's 142-0 win over Namibia at RWC 2003

Right: South Africa's Jannie de Beer kicks one of his record five drop goals in a single match, against England in Paris in 1999

FACTS & STATS

Winning a Rugby World Cup and lifting the Webb Ellis Cup may be the ultimate prize but playing in the Game's global showpiece allows any player or team to write their name in the history books, whether it is a one-off performance or an achievement spanning several Tournaments. The biggest wins, the most points, the youngest try-scorer, the highest attendances, the first red card and much more Rugby World Cup trivia are all contained in this section.

TEAM RECORDS

Biggest victories: top five

Pos	Score	Winner	Opponent	Venue	Date
1	142-0	Australia	Namibia	Adelaide	Oct 25, 2003
2	145-17	New Zealand	Japan	Bloemfontein	Jun 4, 1995
3	101-3	New Zealand	Italy	Huddersfield	Oct 14, 1999
4	111-13	England	Uruguay	Brisbane	Nov 2, 2003
5	108-13	New Zealand	Portugal	Lyon	Sep 15, 2007

Most wins: 37 New Zealand

Most defeats: 21 Japan

Fewest wins: 0 Ivory Coast, Namibia, Portugal, Russia, Spain and Zimbabwe

Most matches without a win:
15 Namibia between 1999 and 2011

Most tries overall: 272 New Zealand

Most points overall: 2,012 New Zealand

Most tries in a match:
22 Australia against Namibia in 2003

Most points in a match:
145 New Zealand against Japan in 1995

Most tries in a single Tournament:
52 New Zealand in 2003

Most points in a single Tournament:
361 New Zealand in 2003

Fewest points in a single Tournament:
14 Romania in 1995

Only team to have played at Rugby World Cup and not scored a try: Spain

Most points scored in a losing cause:
37 Wales in their 53–37 Pool D defeat to New Zealand in 2003

Most tries scored in a losing cause:
5 Wales in their 34–38 defeat to Fiji in Nantes in 2007

Teams failing to score a single point

Score	Team	Opponent	Venue	Date
0-89	Ivory Coast	Scotland	Rustenberg	May 26, 1995
0-20	Canada	South Africa	Port Elizabeth	Jun 3, 1995
0-48	Spain	Scotland	Murrayfield	Oct 16, 1999
0-142	Namibia	Australia	Adelaide	Oct 25, 2003
0-36	England	South Africa	Paris	Sep 14, 2007
0-42	Romania	Scotland	Murrayfield	Sep 18, 2007
0-40	Scotland	New Zealand	Murrayfield	Sep 23, 2007
0-30	Namibia	Georgia	Lens	Sep 26, 2007
0-87	Namibia	South Africa	Auckland	Sep 22, 2011
0-66	Fiji	Wales	Hamilton	Oct 2, 2011

Games decided by a single point

Score	Winner	Opponent	Venue	Date
22-21	Wales	Australia	Rotorua	Jun 18, 1987
19-18	Australia	Ireland	Dublin	Oct 20, 1991
24-23	Ireland	Wales	Johannesburg	Jun 4, 1995
19-18	Fiji	USA	Brisbane	Oct 15, 2003
16-15	Ireland	Argentina	Adelaide	Oct 26, 2003
17-16	Australia	Ireland	Melbourne	Nov 1, 2003
17-16	South Africa	Wales	Wellington	Sep 11, 2011
13-12	Argentina	Scotland	Wellington	Sep 25, 2011
9-8	France	Wales	Auckland	Oct 15, 2011
8-7	New Zealand	France	Auckland	Oct 23, 2011

TRY-SCORING RECORDS

Most tries overall: top ten

Pos	Tries	Player (country, span)
1	15	Jonah Lomu (NZL, 1995-1999)
2	13	Doug Howlett (NZL, 2003-2007)
3=	11	Vincent Clerc (Fra, 2007-2011)
=	11	Chris Latham (Aus, 1999-2007)
=	11	Joe Rokocoko (NZL, 2003-2007)
=	11	Rory Underwood (Eng, 1987-1995)
7=	10	David Campese (Aus, 1987-1995)
=	10	Bryan Habana (RSA, 2007-2011)
=	10	Brian Lima (Sam, 2007-2011)
=	10	Drew Mitchell (Aus, 2007-2011)
=	10	Shane Williams (Wal, 2003-2011)

Leading try-scorers: by Tournament

Year	Player (country)	Tries
1987	Craig Green (NZL)	6
	John Kirwan (NZL)	6
1991	David Campese (Aus)	6
	Jean-Baptiste Lafond (Fra)	6
1995	Marc Ellis (NZL)	7
	Jonah Lomu (NZL)	7
1999	Jonah Lomu (NZL)	8
2003	Doug Howlett (NZL)	7
	Mils Muliaina (NZL)	7
2007	Bryan Habana (RSA)	8
2011	Chris Ashton (Eng)	6
	Vincent Clerc (Fra)	6

Most tries in a match:
6 Marc Ellis (NZL) against Japan at Bloemfontein in 1995

Most tries in a single Tournament:
8 Jonah Lomu (NZL) in 1999
Bryan Habana (RSA) in 2007

First ever Rugby World Cup try:
A penalty try for New Zealand against Italy in the opening match of the 1987 Tournament

Most matches played without scoring a try:
22 Jason Leonard (Eng, 1991-2003)

Youngest try-scorer: George North (Wal) was 19 years 166 days old when he scored two tries against Namibia at New Plymouth on September 26, 2011

Oldest try-scorer: Diego Ormaechea (Uru) was 40 years 13 days old when he touched down against Spain at Galashiels on October 2, 1999

POINTS-SCORING RECORDS

Most points overall: top ten

Pos	Points	Player (country, span)
1	277	Jonny Wilkinson (Eng, 1999-2011)
2	227	Gavin Hastings (Sco, 1987-1995)
3	195	Michael Lynagh (Aus, 1987-1995)
4	170	Grant Fox (NZL, 1987-1991)
5	163	Andrew Mehrtens (NZL, 1995-1999)
6	140	Chris Paterson (Sco, 1999-2011)
7	135	Gonzalo Quesada (Arg, 1999-2003)
8=	125	Matt Burke (Aus, 1995-2003)
=	125	Felipe Contepomi (Arg, 1999-2011)
=	125	Nicky Little (Fij, 1999-2007)

Most points in a match:
45   Simon Culhane (NZL)
     against Japan in 1995

Most points in a Tournament:
126   Grant Fox (NZL) in 1987

Most penalties overall:
58   Jonny Wilkinson (Eng)

Most penalties in a match:
8   Gavin Hastings (Sco) against Tonga
    at Pretoria on May 30, 1995;
    Thierry Lacroix (Fra) against Ireland
    at Durban on June 10, 1995;
    Gonzalo Quesada (Arg) against Samoa
    at Llanelli on October 10, 1999; and
    Matt Burke (Aus) against South Africa
    at Twickenham on October 30, 1999

Most penalties in a Tournament:
31   Gonzalo Quesada (Arg) in 1991

Most conversions overall:
39   Gavin Hastings (Sco)

Most conversions in a match:
20   Simon Culhane (NZL) against Japan
     at Bloemfontein in 1995

Most conversions in a Tournament:
30   Grant Fox (NZL) in 1987

Most drop goals overall:
14   Jonny Wilkinson (Eng)

Most drop goals in a match:
5   Jannie de Beer (RSA) against England
    at the Stade de France in 1999

Most drop goals in a Tournament:
8   Jonny Wilkinson (Eng) in 2003

Most points scored by a player in a losing cause:
24   David Humphreys for Ireland during their
     24–28 defeat to Argentina in 1999

Most points scored by a replacement in a match:
13   Nicky Little for Fiji during their 41–13 victory
     over Japan in 2003

Leading points-scorers: by Tournament

Year	Player (country)	Points
1987	Grant Fox (NZL)	126
1991	Ralph Keyes (Ire)	68
1995	Thierry Lacroix (Fra)	112
1999	Gonzalo Quesada (Arg)	102
2003	Jonny Wilkinson (Eng)	113
2007	Percy Montgomery (RSA)	105
2011	Morné Steyn (RSA)	62

APPEARANCE RECORDS

Most appearances: top ten

Pos	App	Player (country, span)
1	22	Jason Leonard (Eng, 1991-2003)
2	20	George Gregan (Aus, 1995-2007)
3=	19	Jonny Wilkinson (Eng, 1999-2011)
=	19	Mike Catt (Eng, 1995-2007)
5=	18	Lewis Moody (Eng, 2003-2011)
=	18	Martin Johnson (Eng, 1995-2003)
=	18	Mario Ledesma (Arg, 1999-2011)
=	18	Raphael Ibanez (Fra, 1999-2007)
=	18	Brian Lima (Sam, 1991-2007)
10=	17	Aurelien Rougerie (Fra, 2003-2011)
=	17	Jean-Baptiste Poux (Fra, 2003-2011)
=	17	Felipe Contepomi (Arg, 1999-2011)
=	17	John Smit (RSA, 2003-2011)
=	17	Lawrence Dallaglio (Eng, 1999-2007)
=	17	Brian O'Driscoll (Ire, 2003-2011)
=	17	Sean Fitzpatrick (NZL, 1987-1995)

Oldest player:
Diego Ormaechea (Uru) was 40 years 26 days old when he played against South Africa in 1999

Youngest player:
Thretton Palamo (USA) was 19 years 8 days old when he played against South Africa in 2007

Youngest player in a final:
Jonah Lomu (NZL) was 20 years 43 days old when he played against South Africa in the 1995 Final

Youngest Rugby World Cup winner:
François Steyn was 20 years 159 days old when South Africa won the Tournament hosted by France in 2007

Most appearances on the losing side:
11   Romeo Gontineac (Rom, 1995-2007)
     Hugo Horn (Nam, 1999-2011)

Two-time Rugby World Cup winners:
Dan Crowley, John Eales, Tim Horan, Phil Kearns and Jason Little for Australia in 1991 and 1999; Os du Randt for South Africa in 1995 and 2007

Most appearances as captain:
11   Will Carling (Eng, 1991-1995)
     Raphael Ibanez (Fra, 1999-2007)
     Martin Johnson (Eng, 1999-2003)
     John Smit (RSA, 2003-2011)

Jonny Wilkinson holds the record for most points, penalties and drop goals

Number of red cards: by country

3 Canada, Tonga
2 Samoa, South Africa, Wales
1 Argentina, Australia, Fiji, Namibia

Rugby World Cup's first red card:

Huw Richards (Wal) against New Zealand in the 1987 semi-final

Most red cards in a match:

3 South Africa (John Dalton) against Canada (Gareth Rees and Rod Snow) at Port Elizabeth in 1995

Number of yellow cards: by country

10 Tonga
8 France
7 USA
6 Fiji, Italy
5 Argentina, South Africa
4 England, Georgia, New Zealand
3 Australia, Ireland, Namibia, Romania, Samoa
2 Canada, Scotland, Wales
1 Japan, Portugal, Russia

Most yellow cards in a match:

3 **Tonga** (Ipolito Fenukitau and Milton Ngauamo) against **Italy** (Fabio Ongaro) at Canberra on October 15, 2003;
United States (Paul Emerick and Vaha Esikia) against **England** (Lawrence Dallaglio) at Lens on September 8, 2007;
South Africa (Bryan Habana and Francois Steyn) against **Tonga** (Sefa Vaka) at Lens on September 22, 2007;
Argentina (Rimas Alvarez Kairelis and Juan Manuel Leguizamón) against **France** (Raphael Ibanez) at Parc des Princes, Paris, on October 19, 2007;
Tonga (Halani Aulika and Tukulua Lokotui) against **Japan** (James Arlidge) at Whangarei on September 21, 2011

Most yellow cards received by a player overall:

3 Fabio Ongaro (Ita)

Most yellow cards for a team that has gone on to win the match:

2 **Wales** (Colin Charvis and Sonny Parker) during their 41-10 victory over Canada in 2003;
Australia (Drew Mitchell and Nathan Sharpe) during their 32-20 win over Wales in 2007;
South Africa (Bryan Habana and Francois Steyn) during their 30-25 victory over Tonga in 2007;
Argentina (Rimas Alvarez Kairelis and Juan Manuel Leguizamón) during Los Pumas' 34-10 Bronze Final victory over France in 2007;
Tonga (Halani Aulika and Tukulua Lokotui) during the 31-18 victory against Japan in Whangarei in 2011

Rugby World Cup Final referees: by Tournament

Year	Referee (country)
1987	Kerry Fitzgerald (Aus)
1991	Derek Bevan (Wal)
1995	Ed Morrison (Eng)
1999	Andre Watson (RSA)
2003	Andre Watson (RSA)
2007	Alain Rolland (Ire)
2011	Craig Joubert (RSA)

Most matches refereed:

14 Alain Rolland (Ire)

Most matches refereed at one Tournament:

7 Craig Joubert (RSA, 2011)

Number of referees: by country

9 Australia, England
8 New Zealand
7 Ireland, Wales
6 France, South Africa
3 Scotland
2 Argentina
1 Canada, Fiji, Japan, Korea, USA, Samoa

Rugby World Cup-winning coaches: by Tournament

Year	Coach (country)
1987	Brian Lochore (NZL)
1991	Bob Dwyer (Aus)
1995	Kitch Christie (RSA)
1999	Rod Macqueen (Aus)
2003	Clive Woodward (Eng)
2007	Jake White (RSA)
2011	Graham Henry (NZL)

First to play at one Rugby World Cup and coach a team at another:

Daniel Dubroca played for France at the inaugural Rugby World Cup in 1987 and coached them in 1991

Most Tournaments as coach:

3 **Jim Telfer**, Scotland in 1991, 1995 and 1999
Bryan Williams, Samoa in 1991, 1995 and 1999
Graham Henry, Wales in 1999, New Zealand in 2007 and 2011
Nick Mallett, South Africa in 1999, Italy in 2007 and 2011
Eddie O'Sullivan, Ireland in 2003 and 2007, USA in 2011

Player with one team and coach of two different teams:

John Kirwan played for New Zealand in 1987 and 1991 and coached Italy in 2003 and Japan in 2007 and 2011
Pierre Berbizier played for France at Rugby World Cup 1987 and coached France in 1995 and Italy in 2007

Coaching the defending champions:

The best result achieved by a coach leading the defending champions into a Rugby World Cup is to a runners-up finish – by Eddie Jones with Australia in 2003; and Brian Ashton with England in 2007. The worst performance is to reach the quarter-finals – by Bob Dwyer with Australia in 1995 and Peter de Villiers with South Africa in 2011.

Graham Henry coached Wales in 1999 and his native New Zealand in 2007 and 2011, when he finally lifted the Webb Ellis Cup

Rugby World Cup Host Nations

Year	Hosts
1987	Australia and New Zealand
1991	England, France, Ireland, Scotland and Wales
1995	South Africa
1999	Wales
2003	Australia
2007	France
2011	New Zealand

Rugby World Cup Final venues

Year	Venue
1987	Eden Park, Auckland
1991	Twickenham, London
1995	Ellis Park, Johannesburg
1999	Millennium Stadium, Cardiff
2003	Telstra Stadium, Sydney
2007	Stade de France, Paris
2011	Eden Park, Auckland

Longest and shortest duration of Rugby World Cups:

The longest World Cup (by days) is 45 for the 2011 Tournament (Sep 9-Oct 23).

The shortest World Cup was the first, in 1987, which lasted 29 days (May 22-Jun 20)

Most matches hosted by a stadium:

16 Eden Park, Auckland, hosted five matches in 1987 and 11 in 2011. It was also the venue for the inaugural Rugby World Cup Final in 1987 and the most recent in 2011

Highest match attendances: top five

Pos	Spectators	Match	Venue	Date
1	82,957	Australia v England	Telstra Stadium, Sydney	Nov 22, 2003
2	82,444	Australia v New Zealand	Telstra Stadium, Sydney	Nov 15, 2003
3	82,346	England v France	Telstra Stadium, Sydney	Nov 16, 2003
4	81,350	Australia v Argentina	Telstra Stadium, Sydney	Oct 10, 2003
5	80,430	England v South Africa	Stade de France, Paris	Oct 20, 2007

Lowest match attendances: top five

Pos	Spectators	Match	Venue	Date
1=	3,000	Tonga v Ireland	Brisbane	Jun 3, 1987
=	3,000	USA v Romania	Lansdowne Road, Dublin	Oct 9, 1999
=	3,000	Uruguay v South Africa	Hampden Park, Glasgow	Oct 15, 1999
4	3,761	Spain v Uruguay	Galashiels	Oct 2, 1999
5	4,000	Zimbabwe v France	Eden Park, Auckland	Jun 2, 1987

Most matches hosted (by country)

Pos	Matches	Country	Span
1	70	New Zealand	1987-2011
2=	58	Australia	1987-2003
=	58	France	1991-2007
4	32	South Africa	1995
5	20	Wales	1991-2007
6	16	England	1991-1999
7	15	Scotland	1991-2007
8	12	Ireland	1991-1999

Average match attendance: by Tournament

Year	Av. per match	Total spectators	Matches
1987	14,010	448,318	32
1991	33,127	1,060,065	32
1995	29,281	936,990	32
1999	37,965	1,556,572	41
2003	38,263	1,836,607	48
2007	46,786	2,245,731	48
2011	30,743	1,475,688	48

England fans among the record 82,957 spectators at the Telstra Stadium in Sydney for the Rugby World Cup 2003 Final

Piri Weepu leads the Haka before the 2011 Final at Eden Park in Auckland, the ground which has staged most Rugby World Cup matches

Credits

PRESS ASSOCIATION SPORT

Editor   Andrew McDermott

Contributors   Tom Allnutt, Andrew Baldock, Duncan Bech, Steven Birch, Phil Blanche, Cindy Garcia-Bennett, Kate Gardiner, Matt McGeehan, Andy Newport, Ian Parker, Mike Perez, Nick Purewal, Mark Staniforth, Leo Stevens, Martyn Ziegler

Production   Mark Tattersall

Photography   Press Association Images
Except the following:
Action Images: /Adam Holt: 66
Getty Images: /Mike Hewitt: 91; /Chris McGrath: 47TL; /Hannah Peters: 67TL; /David Rogers: 13, 30, 128; /Toru Yamanaka/AFP: 45TL

A ring-tailed lemur gets to grips with a Rugby ball on the Rugby World Cup 2015 Trophy Tour, as part of Land Rover's *Least Driven Path* in Madagascar